KV-243-262

Science in the National Curriculum

Edited by
Mike Watts

CASSELL

Cassell Educational Limited
Villiers House
41/47 Strand
London WC2N 5JE
England

387 Park Avenue South
New York
NY 10016-8810
USA

First published 1991

British Library Cataloguing in Publication Data
Science in the National Curriculum
  1. Great Britain. Schools. Curriculum. Science
  I. Watts, Mike
  507.1041

  ISBN 0-304-32348-9
  ISBN 0-304-32349-7 pbk

Typeset by Colset Private Limited, Singapore
Printed and bound in Great Britain by Biddles Ltd,
Guildford and King's Lynn

Exmouth

University of Plymouth Library

Subject to status this item may be renewed
via your Voyager account

http://voyager.plymouth.ac.uk

Exeter tel: (01392) 475049
Exmouth tel: (01395) 255331
Plymouth tel: (01752) 232323

This book is dedicated to Rhian and Sian

Contents

Preface

It was an afternoon in very early January, 1981, an Association for Science Education conference at the University of Warwick, when I joined a large audience for a debate between Dick West and Mary Waring. Broadly, it was a debate on whether or not science could or should become a compulsory 'core' in the general education of all children. The occasion was vivid because Dick very much caught the mood of the moment and, drawing on his customary rousing eloquence, championed some of the early moves for 'science for all'.

Within the following decade, change has been quite considerable. Science education has been in the van of a wide range of initiatives — political and educational — and in many senses has become the flagship of the National Curriculum. Policy statements have followed statements on policy, review has followed Secondary Science Review, induction and training have followed wherever the money was to be found — and we now have in place a system for a core of science education for all pupils from 5 to 16. It does not perhaps meet all of our hopes and aspirations, nor is it contained within an overall package we might all of us approve — however, we now have 'science for all' in schools.

Of course, while some change has been rapid, some parts of schools and schooling remain seemingly locked for ever in time and space. The images children have of science and scientists: the quirky chemistry teacher, the manic physicists; 'chalk and talk' (and then even more chalk, and more talk); the sights, smells and sounds of school laboratories; the nature table; drawings from MacKean; the Van de Graaff generator; the 'rules of the lab'; and three hundred and one ways to use the Bunsen burner.

But some of that is changing too. Readers who are teachers of science will need little introduction to the now common vagaries and complexities of school science in the years PNC (Post National Curriculum). Science is the fourth 'R' — presumably we now have reading, writing, 'rithmetic and (scientific?) reasoning. And — more importantly — we live with science-across-the-curriculum. As a core subject it has a necessary and fundamental relationship with every other part of the school curriculum. No more can the science curriculum be solely the domain of scientists and the science department — it now belongs in the arena of the whole school.

The National Curriculum Council has delineated five whole-school cross-curricular themes: Economic and Industrial Understanding, Education for Citizenship, Careers Education and Guidance, Health Education, and Environmental Education. These themes are to be seen as part of the basic entitlement for all children in schools and are to be worked alongside and within the core and foundation subject areas. The Council has also indicated three cross-curricular 'dimensions': personal and social development, equal opportunities and multicultural education. These dimensions are more clearly intended to permeate the very fabric of teaching and learning in all areas of school life. The chapters of the book, then, take a slice through the school curriculum. It is a biased view in that we look from the position of the science teacher and how s(he) can begin to tackle the work implied by the meeting of science with the rest of the school.

Within that, our intention here is to produce a text for secondary teachers and for teachers who teach alongside teachers of science and who want to know something about it. The authors joined together in the book are all known to each other in different ways — as friends, colleagues and partners in life. There is an interesting mix of scholarship, managerial skill, advisory expertise and classroom competence, most of which is evident in most of the writing most of the time. Between us we have in mind a sort of 'user's guide' for the classroom practitioner. The book is less about what actually happens in practice at the moment, more about the direction in which things are moving and so towards what she/he/they should be working on in the light of the implications of the National Curriculum: what — in our view — good practice should be. We have not been too concerned with the basics of the 1988 Education

Reform Act, no matter how much it has provoked our approval, annoyance or ennui; we have taken as read that it will be with us in much this form for some time to come. Nor is the text too much of a historical analysis of the last decade leading up to our present state – it is about what needs to be done from this point onwards.

Individually, the chapters are concerned with covering some of the major parts of the secondary curriculum. Not all the areas are here in name, and some readers will note that their own subject is not present at all. No one book can hope to be exhaustive of the school curriculum, and we have taken a route similar to others in the past and considered not the whole curriculum but those 'subject' sections, courses, or 'cross-course' activities we can cope with. So in my own chapter I have bypassed discussions of content in science and focused instead on skills. It is not that content is unimportant, but I feel that discussions of skills, or competencies (core or otherwise) are a growing thread in school life. I am also keen to raise the issue of what pupil entitlement means from the pupils' perspective. It is likely to be a lively debate, so we may as well begin sooner than later. Debbie Zachary looks over the fence at mathematics: traditionally the two areas have not enjoyed the smoothest of relationships, each trying not simply to 'service' the other but retain purity and intrinsic value. Needless to say there are a multitude of ways in which the two areas need to collaborate and Debbie's chapter begins to explore some of these. Jane Ogborn tackles a similar job for English, taking a mixed view of the science curriculum's approach to communications skills. Again the 'service subject' tension needs to be dissipated before both sets of teachers can collaborate on an equitable basis.

Alan West sets out the case for technology as a new subject – not a hybrid rehash of what has gone before. A new subject needs new thinking and he illustrates from his own wealth of experience how this can be (and has been) realized. Gwyn Edwards can find little evidence of any similar movement towards synthesis in the humanities. He paints a complex picture of curricular activity within the usual arms of the 'human sciences' and gives some indications of how scientists can begin to share some of the debate abroad in those areas of the school. Della West provides a lively illustration of how Theatre in Education (TIE) can enrich science classroom activities – and how science can be more 'humanized' through drama.

Di Bentley's chapter explores less the 'warp and weft' of subject-based work than the 'holes' in between, and less how to plug the gaps than how to create a seamless pattern. Her brief is to explore both personal and social education and environmental studies — as in other cases, as seen from the perspective of science. This leads to Pauline Hoyle's chapter on the other National Curriculum dimensions, equal opportunities and multicultural education, where she takes up an increasingly familiar cry of 'opportunities lost' in policy making. Nevertheless, she provides a range of activities and suggested routes to enable the teaching of science. Finally, Dick West and Cathy Wilson explore the routes developing within the morass known as post-16 education. As important as it is for teachers of science to look over the boundaries into other aspects of school work, so it is vital they look over the age-phase wall and ponder the provision in the next stage. We have seen the task of the book as being to help articulate the implications for science across the curriculum (and 16+ age phase), as best we can divine this from the documentation to date and from our own expertise and expectations. So we have tried to be positive and highlight good practice wherever we know it happens, have cited documentation where we know it exists, and been as practical as possible, providing action points and 'checklists' where appropriate. Where necessary, we have been wide-ranging and discussed issues beyond the individual; what the department, faculty and whole school needs to be doing — although the book is addressed ultimately to the classroom teacher. While it may be that advice hinges upon how cross-curricular issues can be raised on agendas, tackled during INSET days, supported by LEA initiatives and so on, we have tried to return the focus to what needs to be done on a middle-term basis. The emphasis, then, is upon curriculum planning and classroom delivery.

On a more recent afternoon, late December 1989 (at the Open University this time), I heard Dick give another lecture on the state of science education. Once more he reached into his bag of words and painted another cogent picture of where school science should be going. It was a cold and crisp evening and on the journey home I kept thinking of how much the style and content of school science had changed in the last ten years — and yet how much more there is to do. The feelings gave me the starting point for this prelude to school science: 'Welcome to science education across the National Curriculum.'

It was an afternoon in very early January, 1981 . . .'.

Notes on Contributors

All the contributors write in their personal capacities and not as representatives of their respective organizations.

Di Bentley is Senior Adviser for Monitoring and Evaluation with Buckinghamshire County Council. After a decade of teaching in inner-city comprehensive schools in Manchester she became Research and Development Officer for Health Education as part of the Secondary Science Curriculum Review. Then, prior to its demise, she was an IBIS Inspector for the Inner London Education Authority. She has written widely in health and science education; her most recent books tackle teaching for active learning, and methods of assessing coursework in science.

Gwyn Edwards spent thirteen years teaching geography and integrated humanities, in schools in Leicester and Kent, before taking his current post as Tutor in Geography Education and Curriculum Studies at Goldsmiths' College, London. He has a keen interest in promoting curriculum development and the professional development of teachers through action research, and at the moment is co-writing a book on curriculum change.

Pauline Hoyle spent ten years working in the inner London area as a science and an ESL teacher and as an advisory teacher. She has experience of working in schools with large numbers of bilingual pupils and in more mixed schools. She has been involved in writing curriculum materials such as Science in Process and Talking Science in which she has contributed her expertise and knowledge of language development and issues of equality. She has been a Multicultural Teacher Fellow at the Institute of Education, London and is a member of the ASE Multicultural Working Party. She is currently an advisory teacher in Surrey.

Jane Ogborn taught English for twelve years in comprehensive schools in inner London before becoming an advisory teacher, and then later an inspector in the ILEA IBIS team. She is now General Inspector with special responsibility for English in Tower Hamlets. She is a GCSE chief examiner in English and is often invited to talk and write about assessment and educational change, particularly as this relates to English and literature.

Mike Watts is Reader in Education at Roehampton Institute, London. From teaching in inner-city comprehensive schools in London and Jamaica, he undertook research at the University of Surrey concerning children's understanding of concepts in physics. With the Secondary Science Curriculum Review he developed interests in many aspects of teaching and learning in science—his current role embraces a broad range of research issues in teacher education. He has published widely and is the author, with colleagues, of books and materials on various aspects of education, most recently books on open-ended problem solving, and small-group work in science.

Alan West is Director of the CREST (Creativity in Science and Technology) Award scheme. Previously he has taught chemistry at a sixth-form centre and has been Head of Science at secondary level. He is author of distance learning materials and articles in science and technology education—and is currently renovating his holiday house is southern France.

Della West teaches drama at secondary level and has been a Head of Drama since the mid-1970s. She is now Learning Manager at her school in Surrey. For the last five years she has also been Project Coordinator of the Science, Technology and Drama Competition for the Surrey SATRO. She has a keen interest in different approaches to teaching and learning through the medium of drama.

Dick West is National Power Professor of Science Education at the Open University. His previous positions include Head of Science at Walworth Comprehensive School in London, Reader in Education at the University of Sussex, Director of the Secondary Science Curriculum Review and Senior Science Inspector at the ILEA. He has written widely within science education and has a keen interest in post-16 education.

Cathy Wilson has taught secondary physics for eight years in the north of England and for some considerable time has been Deputy General Secretary to the Association for Science Education. She was seconded to play an active and important role in the work of the Secondary Science Curriculum Review, and is currently Education Manager for the Institute of Physics. She maintains a strong interest in music – particularly opera and chamber music.

Deborah Zachary has taught physics and mathematics in middle and secondary schools in Bradford and inner London. Her teaching has included periods as Head of Maths, Head of Physics, Head of Science and Head of Sixth Year. She has been an advisory teacher and then inspector for Science in the ILEA, and is currently General Inspector for Tower Hamlets. In her time she has coached and played football professionally in the USA.

Chapter 1

Science across the Curriculum

Mike Watts

STARTING POINTS

> When I was a boy of 14 my father was so ignorant I could hardly
> stand to have the old man around. But when I got to be 21, I was
> astonished at how much he had learned in 7 years.
> (Mark Twain, *'What Is Man' and Other Essays*)

We often view change so personally it becomes difficult to see how
issues appear from other people's perspectives. With hindsight and
some maturity, of course, we can manage all things.

I begin this chapter from the premiss that the 1980s in science
education can be characterized as a period of frenetic development,
but development involving only a small proportion of the teaching
community. I hold the view that the 1990s and the decade after that
augur a time of slower, more cautious consolidation for a far greater
number, and across more age phases within the educational system.
While science education continues to be a key area nationally, in
many ways we are still only at the beginning, and for numerous
science educators little—as yet—has changed. We still have some
growing up to do.

Science in the National Curriculum (DES and Welsh Office, 1989)
is but one part of the legislation enshrined in the Education Reform
Act 1988. My agenda here is to explore some issues in the delivery
of science in the secondary curriculum, not to dissect the Act, con-
done it or rail against it: one way or another it is here to stay for
quite some time.

In general, I take that most readers are conversant with the major features of *Science in the National Curriculum*. The major legal structures and implications are not dealt with — there are many other useful descriptions and discussions of these (see for example Watts, 1990).

VIEWS OF SCIENCE

In some senses I want to turn school science inside out. Can science educators take a sharp look at science and then, viewing from this vantage point, see outwards into other major parts of the school curriculum? The answer must be yes: science education has often led the field, been far-reaching and innovative and is now well equipped both to take stock and to work through the many implications of change.

There are several groups to whom we might address ourselves and whose views should be considered, and I have gathered these broadly into three clusters. First there are all the other teachers and managers within the school. Science teachers are no longer the sole guardians of science, science education is now in the public domain, and it infringes on the work of colleagues and co-professionals. Second, we need to look at science, too, from the pupils' view. They are at the receiving end of what we do, arguably the 'end-point customers' in the enterprise. Third, there is the watching world — the parents, industrialists, LEA officials, HMI and so on. We need to be clear what kind of science scenario we are portraying to our outside audience.

My plan for this chapter is to take only the first, and some small part of the second — the third is beyond the scope of what can be said here. I take the notion of cross-curricular skills as a way of testing the ground for inter-departmental discussion and development, and take a brief moment to consider something of the way pupils see the continuity and coherence of science.

CONVERSATIONS AT WHOLE-SCHOOL LEVEL

There are many points of debate between the department of science and the rest of the school. For example, 'Who does what?'; 'How *much* is done by whom, how and where?'; 'Who in the school is best suited to teaching some aspects of the science curriculum?' and 'Have we the necessary expertise to cover all parts of the programmes of study?' Much of the content of science is open to discussion so that, for example, there is currently debate on exactly where some parts of the science programmes of study might best be taught: in home economics, technology, geography or English? Much of this kind of debate will be taken up in other chapters to follow, and here I want to choose just one slim section of the possible negotiations with colleagues — not content itself, but the teaching of skills. In this sense I want to operate squarely within science profile component 1 (PC 1), which as we go to press is the same as saying New Attainment Target 1 (NAT 1). While the teaching of skills is only one part of the teaching of science, I hope to show that it, too, can be a shared and be a collaborative venture across the curriculum.

The term 'skill' is woolly and vague. The Further Education Unit (FEU, 1982) suggests that skills require perception, decision making, knowledge, judgements and understanding, while also involving some kind of coordinated, overt activity by hands, of speech and so on. They reject, for instance, the notion that a skill is *simply* the ability to perform some manipulative occupational task.

In science, certainly, we see skills as quite complex capacities or competencies. The kinds of skill listed within NAT 1, for instance, are to be able to

plan, hypothesize, predict
design and carry out investigations
interpret results and findings
draw inferences
communicate exploratory tasks and experiments

while in Watts and Michell (1987) we discussed:

processes like:
communicating and discussing, which includes:
questioning, thinking, seeking help, negotiating, listening.
processes of information, which include:

selecting, using relationships, designing, drawing conclusions, controlling interacting variables.
problem solving, experimentation and decision making, which include:
  predicting, inferring, interpreting, formulating hypotheses, modelling, evaluating, assessing, classifying, managing time, costing;
skills like:
  listening, talking, reading, drawing, numeracy, small-group skills, observing, non-verbal communication, searching, measuring, manipulation, graphicacy, recording;
attitudes such as:
  open-mindedness, self-criticism, responsibility, independence of thought, perseverance, cooperation, scepticism, desire to be well informed, confidence, respect, sensitivity, willingness to be involved, tolerance, persuasiveness, questioning, trust.

By adding these processes and attitudes we were trying to signal that skills are not isolated in 'action' but are inseparable from other ongoing activities and value systems.

Rather than try to fix a hierarchy of 'low-order' or 'high-order' skills, it is sometimes preferable to focus on specific and general skills. Some skills may be constrained in their use to a small number of instances, others may be applicable in a variety of contexts. Often skills can be identified in clusters (for instance 'social' skills).

CROSS-CURRICULAR SKILLS

Are there such things as cross-curricular skills? My suggestion here is that, in fact, not only is there a set of skills common to most (all?) areas of school life, but they are fairly specific and not so general as to lose meaning. They are the sorts of skill to which science can easily contribute and therefore form a basis for cross-curricular debate and planning. The list here is my own, but it echoes work that I know is currently taking place in a number of schools:

Organizing and handling information

In science this includes the ability to follow instructions, make plans, extract information, arrange data in sequence, classify, weigh and interpret evidence and draw conclusions, see relationships, make hypotheses, and make the best use of time.

Problem solving

We would normally expect this to mean the ability to diagnose the features and gauge the extent of a problem, to frame hypotheses, design experiments to test them and evaluate the results; the ability to make decisions, draw on relevant ideas and use materials inventively.

Motor skills

This is the realm of physical and practical skills, and might include: the ability to develop and perform tasks requiring manual dexterity and a variety of coordinated body movements, to select appropriate tools and items of equipment and to use them safely and effectively.

Communication

Here we commonly mean the ability to use reading and writing, oral, aural, non-verbal and graphical skills to receive and convey communications, minimizing the risk of misunderstanding. That is, to undertake talking, listening, writing, role play, mime, drama, group skills, graphicacy and display, with particular audiences in mind.

Creativity

This might include the ability to put oneself into other situations, whether of time, place or person, to visualize other experiences; the ability to discipline the imagination by evidence and experience, to reorder and reshape experiences and images. It might involve lateral thinking, composition and spatial awareness.

Numerical skills

The ability to estimate, approximate and measure, and to understand the use of numerical relationships, shape and patterns.

Observation and visual skills

The ability to observe accurately, the ability to record distributions, patterns and relationships, using scale, perspective, shape and colour, and the ability to interpret observations.

Social and personal skills

The ability to cooperate, to negotiate, to express ideas in a variety of contexts, to consider other points of view, to recognize non-verbal communications, to relate to others and demonstrate self-awareness, help make group decisions and undertake leadership roles.

This is not an exhaustive list and some skills might better be subsumed within others; some skills might deserve to be made 'high order' rather than 'lower order'. As mentioned earlier, any discussion of skills is bedevilled by the same concerns — what to some is a 'basic' or 'generic' skill is seen by others as a 'high-order' or 'over-arching' skill. For instance, it can be argued that creativity is not itself a skill and might better be placed inside problem solving or communication; that information handling and communication are the same thing, or that decision making is in fact at the core of all the others. In the end we need to separate out what it is we are looking for in pupil performance, even if there is some duplication and overlap, and this kind of list serves that sort of purpose.

Moving aside for a moment, there are clearly *degrees* of skilfulness, and the assessment of people's skills needs to be done at the appropriate level at which the skill is needed. Consequently, the skills involved in, say, problem solving will depend on the problem, the context in which it is set and the possible routes to a solution. Trying to assess whether or not skills have been deployed successfully will depend on their role in solving the problem.

Any one of the skills above can be spread over a spectrum of performance — on, say, a 5-point scale for assessment (or self-assessment) purposes. So, for example, 'talking' might be described in the following way:

1. is able to give some basic information, relate personal experience and opinion simply, with some hesitation and repetition, when asked;
2. can give basic information and relate personal experience and opinion clearly with some sense of audience;
3. volunteers information clearly. When asked, can be articulate about personal experience and opinion, adapting presentation with a clear sense of context and audience;
4. volunteers complex information in a clear and organized way. Can participate well in group discussions and empathize with other points of view;
5. can initiate sustained discussion and maintain a logical or emotive argument. Can coordinate the discussions of others and synthesize group ideas and debate.

However, in the context of my aims for this chapter, the detail of assessment is something of a digression and is best tackled more fully elsewhere.

SKILLS ACROSS THE CURRICULUM

How well does the list of skills match with other subjects? I think it can be seen quite quickly that there are few areas of the school curriculum which cannot contribute to most — if not all — the general skills in my list. Given that coursework is now often a major (compulsory) part of GCSE, most subject areas entail the handling of data, so that even subjects like physical education and sports studies, which have traditionally focused on physical skills, are taking a full share. The humanities have steadily developed problem-solving approaches within, say, the teaching of history, and the teaching of personal and social skills is rarely the sole domain of Personal and Social Education (PSE) or active tutorial work. Before moving on to talk of the negotiation of the skills curriculum, it is worth making another small digression.

I have explored aspects of problem solving elsewhere (for example, Watts, 1991) and noted that some problems can be developed as good cross-curricular activities to enhance problem-solving skills in many parts of the school. It is a theme I enjoyed immensely within Black and Harrison's (1985) publication *In Place of Confusion* and which has now come to fruition with the publication of the *National Curriculum: Technology* document (DES, 1990). Two such problems might be as follows:

1. Grapes are sometimes partly frozen to concentrate the sugar in the must before being crushed for fermentation. Design and conduct an investigation that looks at the appropriate temperatures of freezing, the origins of the grapes, and the levels of sugar on crushing.
2. Design a way of exploring the effects of feet on the environment. Are those effects greater today than they have ever been?

There are many more such problems, as I described in Watts (1991), and, to a greater or lesser extent, the skills in my list can be incorporated into their solutions. There is a growing trend for these kinds of problem — not necessarily initiated in science — to form the kernel of considerable cross-curricular activity. The CREST project, for instance, described by Alan West in Chapter 4, is a useful illustration of a technological approach to cross-curricular activity.

COMMUNICATING WITH THE REST OF THE SCHOOL

In their discussion of problem solving, Black and Harrison (1985) note that schools

> cannot easily develop the resources within any one department. Neither craft, nor CDT, nor Technology, nor science departments can be expected to equip pupils with the range of resources, knowledge and skills, which they ought to be using in tasks selected to achieve Task-Action-Capability. So collaboration is needed.

Moreover, skills cannot be taught once and be done with — they need to be introduced and practised in simple ways, and then reintroduced and reinforced in several curriculum areas in subsequent school years. Needless to say this needs agreement in principle as well as collaboration in practice, and such a whole-school policy, as Marland (1981) points out, means such issues being firmly rooted in the underlying curriculum plans of the school, absorbed into departmental syllabuses and thence into classroom activities. Such a policy might include:

> statements of aims and objectives and an inventory of the skills which are to be part of the pupils' repertoire. It would specify which teams of teachers were responsible for specific skill areas in each year, offer guidelines on the types of assignments to be given and the resources available, and suggest methods of monitoring the range of assignments set.
>
> (Marland, 1981)

So the question now arises as to how and where the discussions would take place to allow youngsters to tackle these kinds of problems; where the skills involved would best be taught, monitored and assessed.

WITHIN THE DEPARTMENT

As Farmer (1990) points out, in most schools the organization of school departments has evolved only slightly from the departmental structure of the old grammar school system. There is a clear hierarchy of responsibility and (in the jargon of the day) of 'line management'. So, typically, the department may consist of a head of science (possibly a physicist), heads of biology and chemistry, allowances for 'lower-school science' and 'practical assessment', and a main professional grade teacher (not forgetting the student on teaching practice). Of course in smaller or larger schools the hierarchy may be more or less pronounced. Some of the science staff will also have responsibilities in other parts of the school.

With the advent of 'balanced' science and 'technology across the curriculum', departmental structures are changing. Increasingly, the National Curriculum is demanding a revision of responsibilities not within traditional subject areas but on cross-curricular and cross-boundary lines. For example, one trend seems to be a division of responsibility such as a head of science; two teachers then with overall charge for key stages 3 and 4; two further (temporary and movable) allowances for, say, 'Progression across the Stages', 'Assessment', 'Introducing Process Science' or, where appropriate, responsibility for 'key stage 5' (post-16 provision), alongside main professional grade and trainee teachers. Armstrong (1989) and Farmer (1990) also point to the increasing shift towards a faculty structure. For instance, a faculty of science and technology might draw in a sizeable proportion of the school and be composed of various combinations of science, CDT, home economics, art, mathematics, computer studies and business studies: possibly some twelve or thirteen staff in various combinations of permanent, rotating and temporary roles.

It is interesting to note in passing that few other countries in Europe have similar systems. In Germany, for instance, there is no such hierarchy—each teacher of science is still very much an autonomous subject specialist and there is no head of department. Teachers, though, are commonly specialist in two or three diverse subjects (for instance biology and sport; chemistry, mathematics and English) and there is a voluntary (and revolving) chair of conference who chairs the monthly (or so) meeting of science staff. This role involves some reduction in class contact time and is viewed with some esteem, but is a 'collating role' and not a managerial one. That said, the school system in Germany has many other fundamental differences (see, for instance, Hoborough *et al.*, 1990).

What does all this say to individuals within the department? First, it does not do away with subject expertise—that is just as necessary with balanced and cross-curricular science as it is with provision through separate subjects. Schools will still need people who are the 'locus of expertise' even though these same people are teaching across subject disciplines, in much the way that physical education teachers are expected to teach basic fitness, gymnastics, swimming, ball-handling skills, track events or badminton while themselves being specialists in coaching (say) hockey or cricket. Balanced and cross-curricular science does, however, remove subject management issues and shifts divisions of responsibility on to different planes.

Let me go back to my skills-based example. In this case, as the school begins to tackle its 'cross-curricular dimensions', my list of skills (or one like it) becomes the focus for a series of discussions over time. Each member of the department, separately, looks at his or her work and, in joint sessions, illustrates where pupils are encountering or being specifically taught some of the components of the list in lessons. The meetings will inevitably want to show that some special preparation is needed in order to ensure that some of the less traditionally 'science' skills are covered. It is a process similar to that described for other cross-curricular school issues, for example in Watts and Nixon (1989) on health and sex education. It is a process of designing and completing a matrix so that it is easy to see what is done where, by whom and how.

WITHIN LESSONS

The matrix starts with a broad look at the delivery of science in the school. Science is increasingly commonly subdivided into a series of modules. These may follow National Curriculum target titles and be labelled 'variety of life', for instance.

Skills	(A) Information handling	(B) Problem solving	(C) Motor . . .
Modules			
1. Science and scientists			
2. Energy			
3. The variety of living things			
4. The Earth in space			
5. . . . etc.			

So, for example, a module might look at 'the Earth and the solar system' to comply with the key stage 3 programme of study (DES, 1989). This says:

> Pupils should further develop their study of the solar system both by direct naked eye observation and the use of secondary sources. They should consider changes of day length and seasonal changes, chart the passage of time using a sundial, consider ideas about the position of the sun and planets within the solar system, and the position of the solar system in the universe. They should study the extent of human exploration of space.

Here a module will probably have been drawn together within the department and can be used as the basis for debate. Let's say it lasts for seven weeks, given two hours of science per week:

1. Up and down in space
2. Day and night
3. The Earth and its moon
4. The seasons
5. Sol and its system
6. Space and time
7. The known and the unknown

Within the module the need is to ensure that pupils have as many opportunities to develop cross-curricular skills as can be managed. Baxter (1990) describes the wealth of data that indicate how difficult these ideas are for youngsters to grasp, so the skills and content of the module need to be compatible and complementary. One way through the management of the module might be to divide the class into groups (say, seven groups of four) and, after a variety of practical and theoretical sessions, in week 6 to set them different 'problem-solving tasks'. At the very beginning, they are also asked to start collecting data on some aspect of the module for a report-back session in the last lesson of week 7. The week-6 problems could involve building different 'circular' timing devices; investigating sunspots through a 'reversed' telescope; making a sundial; exploring a star-map, and trying to take 'lunar' photographs through a telescope. The week-7 data they collect could include information about the experiments 'left' on the moon after the last visits; what the surface of the moon is like; what the word 'system' means in an astronomical context; what it would be like on Earth if we had two moons of similar size, or one moon twice the size of Luna; what cycles Sol exhibits, and the nature of sunspot activity; why penguins don't fall off the South Pole; what Jupiter's red spot is. They could explain how the sun rises and sets in Australia; describe why there are thirteen months; study the life of Niklas Koppernigk (better known as Copernicus) and so on. The 'data' projects could also be undertaken in groups which might — or might not (not, in my view) — coincide with the problem-solving groups. The final session could be five-minute reports from each group; by mime or role play; by poster session or any other format they chose — with the emphasis on groups choosing an appropriate, creative, vehicle for their work.

'The Earth and the solar system' is just one of (probably) some twenty such modules in key stage 3, with a further ten or so in key stage 4. Such a scheme can then be scrutinized for information handling, problem solving, motor skills, communication, creativity, numerical skills, observation and visual skills, and social group skills as necessary. Each one can be examined for its skill base and in this way the matrix begins to take shape indicating 'how' and 'when' things happen.

WITHIN THE SCHOOL

How then does this matrix become part of the whole-school domain? The notion to resist here is 'If it's done elsewhere in the school, then we don't have to do it!' The consolidation, variation, security and reinforcement of skills in each area of the school is the vital point. What's more, it will need more than one whole INSET day to sort through the issues. As much as the English department may want to retain dominant control of communication skills, they will also need to come to terms with tackling – and assessing – the act of problem solving in their own lessons. Just as the science department will have learn how to teach and assess information-handling skills in their sessons, so they must prepare to teach school colleagues in history or religious education how to undertake direct skill teaching for practical motor skills and/or numerical manipulation. Let us be quite clear, the module on 'The Earth and the solar system' has a strong impact on both those particular subject areas, and the teachers there need to know – and understand – what is happening in science.

Discussions and debates about cross-curricular skills are long and complex. For instance, if there are eight other curriculum areas in the school, it would take seven separate meetings for the science department to reach an overall view of what is taking place elsewhere and how its own work might relate to the work of the whole school. An alternative would be for someone in each department or faculty to hold a 'cross-curricular brief' so they could report on the planning with other departments. It would mean having someone, too, from each of the other major departments along to science department meetings each time.

Moreover, the communal departmental filing cabinet would need sections similar, perhaps, to the chapter titles in this book: the interactions of science and mathematics, science and English, science and technology; the skills for the modules; the assessment packages and their relationships to national assessment needs. As much as anything, it would take considerable INSET time for science teachers to gain familiarity with other subject areas and ways of thinking.

AT PUPIL LEVEL

Let me, for a moment, leave departmental and inter-departmental structures and strictures and take a view of science from the inside out, from the customer point of view. In this final part of the chapter I want to look at some of the comments made by pupils and what this might mean for cross-curricular science.

What do young people in schools want their science education to be? How would *they* have it? In Ebbutt and Watts (1987), we were given a very clear picture: science in school should be relevant; have coherence and continuity; be responsive to individual needs and help foster genuine enquiry. Not too much to ask, at first glance. Our interviews with 17-year-olds in school, however, left us in no doubt that their actual experiences of science from 11 to 16 had been somewhat less than this — that is, generally irrelevant; lacking continuity and coherence; impervious to personal predilection, and short of the excitement born of discovery and exploration. Nor were these views solely those of sixth-form sceptics; we received similar opinions with younger pupils in other contexts (see Bentley, 1986; Watts and Bentley, 1986), though no doubt a full-scale enquiry would unearth counter-views and minority opinions.

We can all of us argue the million or so reasons why schools and schooling (of all kinds) cannot meet all consumer demands, not least of which is being caught in a strangulating grip between constantly rising expectations and increasingly restricted resources. As one local councillor recently noted proudly, his education authority was close to the top of the league in examination results while being one of the lowest spenders on education. How to make the top of the results league? Why, spend even less on schools, he said in all seriousness.

The points made by these youngsters have a certain 'ring of truth' about them and I use them here to lead a discussion in what might be done:

> *Robert*: We did, say, chapter 11, then chapter 3, and we got things in chapter 11 we had not covered yet, so it was just confusing. . . .
> *Steve*: . . . and each different practical didn't have much connection to the last.
> *Andrew*: We did our physics in sort of separate sections in no apparent order.
> *Alice*: Yes, they ought to relate it more, in some sort of order. I mean one minute we had to do reproduction and the next we were doing paper chromatography. . . .
>
> (a group discussion, from Ebbutt and Watts, 1987)

What does it take to design a science curriculum which is both coherent and continuous? One problem with the layout of skills and content of traditional science, and potentially for science in the National Curriculum, is that it can lead to actual provision being fragmented and 'bitty': 'Today, Class 6, we'll do information handling skills through Attainment Target 5, level 4, statement b; tomorrow it's problem solving in AT 7, level 5 statement c . . .', and so on. While we will never eradicate the perennial cry 'We've already done that, Miss', we must strive not to plug the gaps but to provide a clear and well-framed picture.

One argument for the National Curriculum is that – at last – we have some public indication of what might be taught in science in schools. The picture is thus provided for us and I know more schools than one where the science department has turned the programmes of study into 'pupilspeak' and put key words around the walls in the form of a display. Like it or not the continuity and coherence of school science lies in our interpretations of the document. Consequently the kinds of module discussed before, and the range of skills outlined earlier, form part of an overall agenda for pupils' science that needs to be made clear (and to make sense) to them. In this way does another pupil, Marcello, see it:

> I think this is one of the biggest problems . . . you come into the classroom and few teachers give you an introduction relating to the topic they're going to teach and how it relates to other stuff. And you have to go home and read your notes to realize what it means. I mean, I think the whole approach to teaching is a little wrong because you get like one thing then on top of that another thing . . . it's not the way that science history is, really. Science is like a spider's web, it

kind of spreads out, it makes sense in a wider scope. But when you're being taught, you know, you have to really work hard to relate it to anything . . .

But the problem now grows to that of coherence and continuity not just across biology, chemistry and physics (plus earth sciences and astronomy) but across all other subjects as well. Until now, schools have been unable to view the curriculum horizontally, across all secondary courses — this is really where the debate begins.

In their most positive light, the National Curriculum programmes of study are a statement of the curriculum entitlement for all young people aged 5–16. In the discussions and debates on the provision of science across the curriculum we must not lose sight of individual 'pupil tracks' — the menu of experiences as seen through the eyes of individuals. *Technology: Non-Statutory Guidance* (NCC, 1990) comes closest of all the recent curriculum documents to reinforcing this point. It provides four brief (fictional) cameos of Alex, Sunita, Jan and Jenny which are reminiscent of ones written for science by the Secondary Science Curriculum Review in 1984 (SSCR, 1984). The point is to give some idea of how provision can be woven together to provide a coherent and continuous cloak of experience — not just within science but across the school curriculum.

FINAL COMMENTS

There are many more aspects to school science than the skills pupils need or the necessary coherence of the content. Without, for instance, a continuous supply of high-quality teachers all will be for naught — and the future prospects are none too bright. However, in highlighting skills, and attempting to consider something of the pupils'-eye view, I have attempted to hold open an avenue for discussion between subjects and courses in the whole-school curriculum.

REFERENCES

Armstrong, R. (1989) The joys (mostly) of running a balanced science faculty. *Change in Focus*, **4** (Summer). York: National Curriculum Council for the Secondary Science Curriculum Review.

Baxter, J. (1990) Children's understanding of familiar astronomical events: potential for the school science curriculum. Paper presented to the British Educational Research Association Conference, London, September, for the Children's Learning in Science Project, University of Leeds.

Bentley, D. (1986) Less theory, more enterprise: some girls' view of science education. Paper presented to the British Psychological Society Conference, London.

Black, P. and Harrison, G. H. (1985) *In Place of Confusion*. London: Nuffield/Chelsea Curriculum Trust; Nottingham: Trent Polytechnic.

DES [Department of Education and Science] and the Welsh Office (1989) *Science in the National Curriculum*. London: HMSO.

DES [Department of Education and Science] and the Welsh Office (1990) *Technology in the National Curriculum*. London: HMSO.

Ebbutt, D. and Watts, D. M. (1987) *Science Is like a Spider's Web*? Hatfield, Herts: Association for Science Education for the Secondary Science Curriculum Review.

Farmer, R. (1990) The management of science departments in secondary schools. *Education Today*, **40**(1), 27-9.

FEU (1982) *Basic Skills*. Further Education Curriculum Review and Development Unit, London.

Hoborough, J., Pope, M. L. and Watts, D. M. (1990) The rise and fall(?) of the Euro-teacher: a case study report on the Oldenburg/Surrey project. Paper presented to the British Educational Research Association Annual Conference Symposium 'Science Education Research in an International Context', Roehampton Institute, London, 30 August-2 September.

Marland, M. (1981) (ed.) Information skills in the secondary curriculum. *Schools Council Curriculum Bulletin*, **9**. London: Methuen.

NCC [National Curriculum Council] (1990) *Technology: Non-Statutory Guidance*. York: National Curriculum Council.

SSCR [Secondary Science Curriculum Review] (1984) Towards a specification of minimum entitlement: Brenda and friends. *Secondary Science Curriculum Review*. London: Schools Curriculum Development Committee.

Watts, D. M. (1990) The science curriculum. In *Manual for Heads of Science*. London: Croner Press.

Watts, D. M. (1991) *The Science of Problem Solving*. London: Cassell.

Watts, D. M. and Bentley, D. (1986) Down the tubes: viewers' opinions of science education television in the classroom. *School Science Review*, **69** (248), 451-9.

Watts, D. M. and Michell, M. (1987) *Choosing Content. Better Science: Curriculum Guide 2*. London: Heinemann and ASE for Secondary Science Curriculum Review, and Schools Curriculum Development Committee.

Watts, D. M. and Nixon, J. (1989) *A Whole School Policy for Health and Sex Education*. Basingstoke: Macmillan Educational.

Chapter 2

Science and the Mathematics Curriculum

Deborah Zachary

INTRODUCTION

Science and mathematics have traditionally shared an uncomfortable space in the school curriculum. The old divisions in which mathematicians complain that scientists treat mathematical topics with methods that limit the pupils' understanding, while scientists treat mathematics as a service industry and complain that the pupils' mathematical skills are not good enough for their science, have often become more marked where mathematics departments have introduced modern methods or moved towards individualized learning systems.

The advent and concurrent production of the National Curricula for mathematics and for science provide an opportunity for the subjects to cooperate within a clearly defined framework. A pupil now has an entitlement in law not only to a broad and balanced science education, but also to a mathematics syllabus spanning traditional and modern, basics and practical applications. Important, too, from the teacher's point of view is the fact that the curricula are far more permanent than individual departmental schemes of work. Time spent now in cross-curricular INSET and planning is guaranteed to be returned in time saved over several years.

It is perhaps worth rehearsing here the arguments for closer links between mathematics and science in terms of benefits for the pupil. Both science and mathematics have made attempts in recent years to become more 'child centred' in their approach. In mathematics this has resulted in more investigatory work and individualized

learning, and most recently in the National Curriculum in the inclusion of applications of mathematics. In science, practicals moved towards investigations and again into an emphasis on application. Other projects have gone further: for example the Children's Learning in Science Project (CLISP, 1990) sees pupils as partners in the learning process and has emphasized the need to work from the place where the individual pupils start rather than the place the teacher thinks they should be. The Raising Achievement in Mathematics Project (RAMP, 1990) stresses pupils' responsibility and aims to equip them to solve real mathematical problems for themselves rather than through adopting 'model answers'. The message coming through is that real education is about equipping pupils to use their skills in real contexts, and that skills taught in isolation are likely to remain bound within that single context for pupils. In school the curriculum can appear fragmentary. At least if science and mathematics teachers have some familiarity with each other's schemes and methodology, the implicit message given to pupils is one of security, that staff are not excluding all other aspects of the work the pupil does.

The intention of this chapter is twofold: to analyse the points of contact between the National Curricula in the two subjects, and to make suggestions for action at various levels within the school. It should be noted that the emphasis throughout is on Attainment Targets rather than programmes of study. This is not from any endorsement of an assessment-led mode of operation, but simply for ease of reference. A particular item is indicated through writing target number, subject, level and then statement as necessary in that order. For example, '2Sc3a' indicates the first statement of attainment on level 3 of the science Attainment Target 2, '2Sc3' indicates the whole of the level, and '2Sc' the whole of the target (DES, 1989).

ANALYSIS OF THE NATIONAL CURRICULA

The National Curriculum in mathematics has 14 Attainment Targets divided by content into two profile components. (The first component, of 8 Attainment Targets covers number, algebra and measures, while the second moves on to shape and space and data handling.) Each profile component has an Attainment Target (numbers 1 and 9) concerned with 'using and applying mathematics' and it is here that perhaps the greatest scope for cooperation lies. Comparing the statements of attainment from 1Ma or 9Ma (they are the same) with some of those from 1Sc immediately highlights the subjects' shared concerns (1Ma/9Ma extracts are given first in each case, then the 1Sc extracts, indented):

3a   select the materials and mathematics to use for a task; check results and consider whether they are sensible.

      3d   select and use simple instruments . . .

3b   explain work being done and record findings systematically.

      3f   record experimental findings . . .

      3i   describe activities carried out . . .

3c   make and test predictions.

      3a   formulate hypotheses . . .

4a   select the materials and the mathematics to use for a task; plan work methodically.

      4d   plan an investigation . . .

      4e   select and use a range of measuring instruments . . .

4b   record findings and present them in oral, written or visual form as appropriate.

      4h   record results . . .

      4j   describe investigations . . .

4c   use examples to test statements or definitions.

      4c   construct 'fair tests'.

5a   select the materials and the mathematics to use for a task; check there is sufficient information; work methodically and review progress.

5b   interpret mathematical information presented in oral, written or visual form.

5c   make and test simple statements.

      5a   use concepts, knowledge and skills to suggest simple questions and design investigations to answer them.

      5c   select and use measuring instruments . . .

      5d   make written statements of the patterns . . .

6a   design a task and select appropriate mathematics and resources; check there is sufficient information and obtain any that is missing; use 'trial and improvement' methods.

6b use oral, written or visual forms to record and present findings.

6c make and test generalizations and simple hypotheses; define and reason in simple contexts with some precision.

> 6 contribute to the analysis and investigation of a collaborative exercise in which . . .
> each pupil should:
> a use experience and knowledge to make predictions in new contexts.
> c prepare a detailed written plan . . .
> d record data in tables and translate it into appropriate graphical forms.
> e produce reports which include a critical evaluation . . .

7a devise a mathematical task; work methodically within an agreed structure; use judgement in the use of given information; use 'trial and improvement' methods; review progress.

> 7 plan, design and safely carry out an entire investigation . . .

7b follow a chain of mathematical reasoning, spotting inconsistencies; follow new lines of investigation using alternative approaches.

8a devise a mathematical task and make a detailed plan of the work; work methodically, checking information for completeness; consider whether the results are of the right order.

8b make statements of conjecture using 'if . . . then . . .'; define, reason, prove and disprove.

> 8b make generalizations from several data sets . . .

9a design, plan and carry through a mathematical task to a successful conclusion.

9b state whether a conjecture is true, false or not proven; define and reason; prove and disprove and use counter-examples; use symbolization; recognize and use necessary and sufficient conditions.

> 9 in the context of an extended investigation . . .
> a [research . . . !
> b [plan . . . !

c   [interpret . . . !
d   [draw conclusions . . . !
e   [present . . . !

10a   design, plan and carry through a mathematical task to a successful conclusion; present alternative solutions and justify selected route.

10b   give definitions which are sufficient or minimal; use symbolization with confidence; construct a proof using proof by contradiction.

10   in the extended investigation . . .
a   evaluate critically . . .
b   suggest alternatives . . .

A scientist's immediate thought might be that all of these mathematical statements of attainment could be delivered in the context of a scientific investigation. The concern of a mathematics department, however will be to ensure that these processes are applied to all areas of mathematics, and that will demand a wider angle of approach than the subjects of science alone. Even if it were possible to cover all these areas of mathematics through science, everyday life obviously demands the application of mathematics across a much wider spectrum. Alternatively, scientists might like to reflect how much of 1Sc is covered by a mathematical investigation. An example is included at the end of the chapter (Figure 2.2).

Although scientists must be forewarned not to assume too great an importance for their subject in a mathematical context, I would expect mathematical colleagues to welcome suggestions that will help them map the occasions when science could be used as an application. Similarly, scientists need to know what levels of mathematics link to, or are prerequisites for, the work they plan. Table 2.1 links some major cross-references between the two subjects, in addition to those already pointed out.

This kind of analysis should not be regarded as definitive. Science teachers will recognize that there are many aspects of their National Curriculum in which the actual nature of achievement expected is not clear: is there a distinction between a level 5 'understand' and a level 7 'understand', apart from the content, for example? There are similar aspects, though not so many examples, in the mathematics document. It seems likely that only by a process of teaching and

Table 2.1   *Cross-references between the science and mathematics National Curricula*

Sc ref	Subject	Links to/ requires	Ma ref
1Sc3e	Measuring		8Ma3b
1Sc3fg	Tables/Bar charts		13Ma2a,3a
1Sc4e	Select instruments		8Ma3b
1Sc4h	Bar charts/Line graphs		13Ma3a,4c
1Sc6d,e	Reporting, graphs		8Ma6b, 12Ma6a, 13Ma4,5,6
1Sc7c	Appropriate recording methods		12Ma6a,7ab, 13Ma4,5,6,7
2Sc3b	Sorting		13Ma2b
2Sc5b	Keys		13Ma4a
3Sc10	Metabolic processes		13Ma7b
4Sc4a	Measurement		8Ma3ab,4a
4Sc7a,8ab	Genetics		14Ma6a,6b
6Sc4c	Volume		8Ma4a
6Sc6c	Density		8Ma6a
6Sc8a	Volume/Pressure		7Ma8a
7Sc8a	Rates of reaction		2Ma6b, 3Ma6b
8Sc9d,10d	Half-life		5Ma9
9Sc8a	Geological timescale		2Ma8a
10Sc6a	Speed		8Ma6a
10Sc6b	Pressure		2Ma6b, 3Ma6b
10Sc9a	$F=ma$		6Ma8a
10Sc10a	Formulae in new situations		6Ma10a
11Sc8a	Resistance		6Ma8a, 8Ma6a
13Sc7b	Efficiency		2Ma6b, 3Ma5b,6b 6Ma8a
13Sc9a	Work/energy calculations		6Ma8a
15Sc3b	Investigating mirrors		10Ma4a
15Sc4b	Shadows		11Ma6c
15Sc5	Reflection		11Ma6b
15Sc6a	Prisms/Lenses		10Ma6a,5b
15Sc8a	Wave velocity: refraction		2Ma6b, 3Ma6b
16Sc3a	Inclination of sun		10Ma4a
16Sc4b	Scale of solar system		8Ma4c
17Sc5b	Patterns & alternatives		5Ma4b

NOTE: In addition to this, 4Ma concerning number, calculators and estimation applies across a large number of the science targets.

Ma ref	Subject	Is applied in	Sc ref
2Ma6b	Ratio		7Sc8a, 10Sc6b, 13Sc7b, 15Sc8a
2Ma8a	Standard index form		9Sc8a
3Ma5b	Percentage		13Sc7b
3Ma6b	Ratio		7Sc8a, 10Sc6b, 13Sc7b, 15Sc8a

Table 2.1 (*contd*)

Ma ref	Subject	Is applied in	Sc ref
4Ma	Calculation, estimation		1Sc + many others
5Ma4b	Generalized patterns		1Sc5d, 17Sc5b
5Ma9	Growth/decay rates		8Sc9d,10d
6Ma8a	Manipulate formulae		10Sc9a, 11Sc8a, 13Sc7b,9a
6Ma10a	Formulae in new contexts		10Sc10a
7Ma8a	Reciprocal functions		6Sc8a
8Ma3a	Metric units		4Sc4a
8Ma3b	Choosing instruments		1Sc3e,4e, 4Sc4a
8Ma4a	Relations between units		4Sc4a, 6Sc4c
8Ma4c	Estimates of measures		16Sc4b
8Ma6a	Compound measures		6Sc6c, 10Sc6a, 11Sc8a
8Ma6b	Approximation and accuracy		1Sc6d,e
10Ma4a	Angle language		15Sc3b, 16Sc3a
10Ma5b	Angle properties		15Sc6a
10Ma6a	Angles and polygons		15Sc6a
11Ma6b	Reflection		15Sc5
11Ma6c	Enlargement		15Sc4b
12Ma6a	Collect data		1Sc6d,e,7c
12Ma7a	Collect data		1Sc7c
12Ma7b	Record data		1Sc7c
13Ma2a	Block graphs		1Sc3fg
13Ma2b	Classifying (two criteria)		2Sc3b
13Ma3a	Bar charts		1Sc3fg,4h
13Ma4a	Decision tree-diagram		2Sc5b
13Ma4c	Line graph		1Sc4h
13Ma4,5,6	Recording		1Sc6de,7c
13Ma7b	Flow diagrams		3Sc10
14Ma6a	Outcomes of two events		4Sc7a,8ab
14Ma6b	Several outcomes		4Sc7a,8ab

assessment over several years will a consensus be reached, and that consensus will illuminate further links between the two subjects. For the moment I have assumed that it is not worth while to list connections which span more than one or two levels, however obvious (e.g. 10Sc9b: kinetic energy and 2Ma5a: index notation); or to assume too much depth in a science statement of attainment (e.g. 10Sc4a: size and direction of forces which otherwise would need 11Ma8b: vectors).

THE WAY FORWARD

In terms of the cross-referencing, then, how can the two subject areas work together for the benefit of the child from the point of view of both schemes of work and teacher assessment? Liaison at the level of the planning for schemes of work is fairly clear-cut. There are two aspects to it, which might be entitled 'mathematics in science' and 'science in mathematics'.

Mathematics in science

The traditional concern of scientists has been that pupils often 'do not have the mathematical skills they need'. If scientists feel that this is the case, it is worth looking further into the matter to see why the situation is arising.

It may indeed be that, for some reason, in a particular school or class children are not progressing adequately in mathematics. Alternatively, the scenario may be more complex. Major difficulties can often arise through differences in approach between the subjects. I have talked to pupils who thought that equations in physics were radically different from equations in mathematics. After all, physics equations were about lots of quantities you measured, and you found an unknown by 'swapping' figures from one side to the other, following careful rules about changing signs. In mathematics, though, you dealt with an 'x', and you either used flow charts to find out what the 'x' meant, or else you used the idea of a pair of scales, doing the same thing to both sides to keep it balanced. At a more trivial level there can be a difference in the approach to calculators. A mathematics department might have a class set easily available, whereas pupils were expected to provide their own or share in science. The mathematics used in science then immediately appears harder, or at least less interesting. It is also possible that a science department might be teaching mixed-ability classes through exposing pupils to the same sort of inputs and expecting to be able to differentiate by outcome. In the same school the mathematics department might be running an individualized learning system like 'SMILE', in which pupils learn new mathematical concepts at a time which is right for them as individuals. The result may be that some pupils will not have the necessary mathematical skills to join in a science activity because, in fact, they are not ready to acquire them. In that case, it is the science department who should look again at the strategies they are using.

These are difficult issues, but the first step is for science teachers to familiarize themselves with the method of work of the mathematics department. In a traditional school, where mathematics is taught to classes set by ability and a class scheme of work is followed, a mapping exercise could be the first step to coherent and cross-referenced programmes. In a school in which the mathematics department has moved on to a more individualized approach, science teachers can at least familiarize themselves with the mathematical level of the pupils they teach. In any situation, however, a discussion of mathematical methodology is essential. If scientists, at the end of such a discussion, feel that they need to develop pupils' mathematics further they can at least start from the same groundwork. An example of this (Figure 2.1) might be in the context of work with equations, mentioned earlier. Some other examples are to be found in Zachary (1989).

The key is to enable pupils to relate any method they have acquired, and any mathematical skills they have developed, to the work they do in science. Discussions with the mathematics department or with pupils will suggest areas in which 'modern' approaches may be different from those of the science teacher, and some other examples are listed below:

- approaches to rotational and reflective symmetry
- enlargement using scale factors
- use of equivalent fractions
- inverse operations
- a great variety of methods for calculations without calculators
- mapping diagrams

Science in mathematics

Mathematics teachers would benefit from any discussions of science schemes of work which enable them to refer to science for practical examples of mathematics. As well as this, there are often occasions when pupils are working on small projects or homework, or even in the course of a lesson, when one or two become particularly interested and want to pursue a topic further. If the work involves links to mathematics the liaison can prove very fruitful. It might be possible to put aside one or two lessons from both subject areas each

Problem: find t in $v = u + at$ if $v = 26$ m s^{-1}, $u = 2$ m s^{-1} and $a = 4$ m s^{-2}.

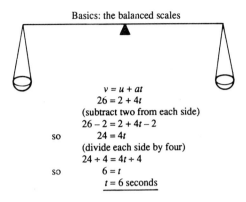

Basics: the balanced scales

$$v = u + at$$
$$26 = 2 + 4t$$
(subtract two from each side)
$$26 - 2 = 2 + 4t - 2$$
so $\quad 24 = 4t$
(divide each side by four)
$$24 \div 4 = 4t \div 4$$
so $\quad 6 = t$
$$\underline{t = 6 \text{ seconds}}$$

Method 1: 'swapping' sides (the link with the above should be made clear).

$$26 = 2 + 4t$$
$$26 - 2 = 4t$$
(+2 becomes -2 as it is moved)
$$24 = 4t$$
$$24 \div 4 = t$$
($\times 4$ becomes $\div 4$ as it is moved)
$$6 = t$$
$$\underline{t = 6 \text{ seconds}}$$

Method 2: flow chart

$$26 = 2 + 4t$$
show how the right-hand side is built up

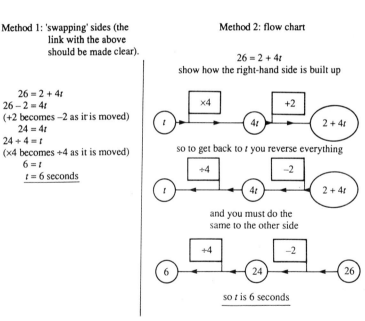

so to get back to t you reverse everything

and you must do the same to the other side

so t is 6 seconds

Figure 2.1 Illustration of methods of solving an equation

term or half term for pupils to work on a project that spanned the two disciplines. The projects might be chosen by pupils or teachers, and could involve work at a variety of levels to suit individual pupils or groups. The detail would have to be worked out at school level, but a few of the many starting points are listed here:

- using unusual methods to report findings in an investigation, e.g. methods used to prepare salts (1Sc7, 6Sc5bc, 7Sc6a, 7Sc8a, 13Ma7b, 9Ma6b)
- designing a periscope or other machines involving mirrors (1Sc4fgj,5a, 15Sc4,5,6a, 9Ma4ab, 10Ma4ab,5b)
- investigating electricity consumption in the home (11Sc6d, 13Sc5a,6b,7c, 2Ma4e,5b,6ab, 8Ma6ab)

ASSESSMENT

Project work links between the two subjects suggest possibilities for a common approach to assessment. It might be that the same project provides evidence for statements of attainment in both subjects, but that the work is assessed separately by science and mathematics staff. Alternatively, where the statements of 1Sc match 1/9Ma very closely, it might be possible for an assessment made by one teacher to be used in another subject area. This, after all, is effectively what happens at key stages 1 and 2. There are potential pitfalls in terms of being sure that the processes listed in the statements of attainment are actually being applied to the correct subject area for the assessment, and in terms of the ability of a non-specialist to make those assessments in a specialist application. These are matters for the individual school to look at, and structures would have to be set up within the individual school to support any developments of this sort.

SUMMARY OF SUGGESTED ACTION

The whole-school context

There are a variety of implications for closely cooperative work at key stages 3 and 4. They can be addressed in a variety of ways — in whole-school INSET, by working parties, or at senior management level, for example. They include the following aspects:

- if different departments are to share the work of teacher assessments in one National Curriculum subject, the school will have to make careful arrangements for moderation and for the keeping of 'evidence'
- the question of a common marking and record-keeping policy may need to be addressed
- extra preparation time may be needed
- whole-school INSET time might be allocated for cross-curricular use
- cross-curricular work will have to be well documented for the purposes of completion of schedule 1 (the DES curriculum return)

The department

The extent of action for the department depends on the amount of cross-curricular work to be generated. It is suggested that the following programme might be followed:

1. Departmental discussions and analysis of schemes of work could take place in order to draw out the aspects of mathematics currently involved in science.
2. A series of INSET sessions could be held with members of the mathematics department. (It would be possible to pursue these issues in smaller meetings, for example between the two subject heads, but probably less productive.) ˋ
   (a) Awareness raising: National Curriculum: 1 hour
       − brief presentations/workshops for each department on the National Curriculum in the other subject.
   (b) Awareness raising: processes: 1 hour
       − a useful start is to get each department to complete the sentence 'pupils are doing science (mathematics) when they are — ing' (e.g. investigating, reading, etc.) for their own subject. Then exchange lists and cross off words which apply to the other subject as well: not many are likely to remain. This could lead into a comparison of 1Sc and 1/9Ma.

    (c)   Mathematical methods: 1 hour
         — this INSET should be led by members of the mathematics department. Its form will depend on policies followed in a particular school, but would be likely to include aspects such as equations, methods of calculation and so on.

    (d)   Either: mapping: half-day
         or: mathematics learning system: half-day
         — it may be possible to map the mathematics scheme of work against that of the science department in order to look for overlap, and perhaps make some revisions to give pupils a more rational programme. If the mathematics department follows a more individualized learning approach, then time would be well spent on giving the science department an induction into the system, classroom procedures and record keeping, even to the extent of allowing them to try out work.

The individual teacher

To some extent the possibilities open to the individual teacher are governed by departmental policies. Nevertheless, with or without departmental involvement, there are a series of useful steps to take.

1.   Make sure you are familiar with the mathematics scheme in operation at your school. Is it an individual scheme, or is it taught to whole classes at a time? Are classes 'set' by ability? What sorts of teaching strategy are used? What records are kept? Think about the same questions in relation to your own lessons and imagine how a pupil has to adjust from one subject to another.

2.   Find out what mathematical methods are used by pupils for things like equations and calculations. You could talk to a colleague, or ask the children directly in a lesson as the context arises.

3.   Try a mathematical investigation for yourself (see Figure 2.2).

4.   Track down your pupils — what mathematics class are they in? What level is their mathematical competence in the eyes of the 'experts'?

This is an equilateral triangle.

There is only one way of arranging one triangle, and only one way of arranging two triangles so that their sides touch.

(Turning it by rotating it does not make it different!)

Here are some examples of ways for four triangles:

Try 3 triangles, 5 triangles, more . . .

Is there a pattern?

Figure 2.2 A sample mathematical investigation

5. It may be possible to plan a short joint project with a colleague who teaches your pupils mathematics. This benefits you as well as the colleague in that you acquire a good deal of operational knowledge of the other department.

Possibilities for action *are* dependent on your own school situation, but benefits to pupils will result even if contacts are only at the level of discussions of methodology. Even if these have taken place in the past it may be that now is a suitable moment to reopen them, in the light of the new curricula. There may be unexpected benefits too. Teachers might find their own interest in mathematics renewed as they discover some of the changes that have taken place in the subject. The investigation that concludes this chapter serves a variety of purposes, including simply that of an example, but readers may find it an interesting exercise for its own sake. The investigation is open-ended, and pupils will reach different levels of achievement.

• Some will ask for equipment — scissors, dotted paper, tracing paper . . .

- Some will just draw triangles
- Some will arrange their drawings in order
- Some will summarize their results in a table
- Some will summarize their results in a sentence, talking about the way the numbers change
- Some will predict the next result and then test their prediction, operating within the rules of the investigation
- Some will write a report on their work
- Some will write a conclusion in words
- Some will work together to get more results
- Some will generalize their results to an algebraic expression or rule
- Some will criticize their work and look for alternatives

How many statements of attainment from Attainment Target 1 in science will be satisfied?

REFERENCES

CLISP [Children's Learning in Science Project] (1990). Mimeograph c/o Dr Rosalind Driver, CSSME, University of Leeds.

DES [Department of Education and Science] and Welsh Office (1989) *Science in the National Curriculum*. London: HMSO.

RAMP [Raising Achievements in Mathematics Project] (1990). Mimeograph c/o The Mathematics Centre, West Sussex Institute of Higher Education, Bognor Regis.

SMILE is a curriculum project originally set up by the ILEA. Details from The SMILE Centre, Kensal Rd, Ladbroke Grove, London W10.

Zachary, D. (1989) Mathematics in physics education. *Physics Education*, **24**(6), 21-8.

Chapter 3

Science and English

Jane Ogborn

As an English teacher — or, more importantly in this context, as someone whose main concern is with school students as developing and increasingly competent and confident users of language — I find a lot to welcome in the science National Curriculum documents, *Science in the National Curriculum* (DES and Welsh Office, 1989) and *Science: Non-Statutory Guidance* (NCC, 1989). But I also find a lot that worries me. The parts I welcome are those which recognize that language and communication are central to the processes of learning. The parts that worry me are those which seem to be based on assumptions that this interdependence of aspects of language and communication and the processes by which children learn science and demonstrate what they have learned might be simple and unproblematic. Much in these documents seems to assume that students come to science with the communicative skills needed to demonstrate their knowledge and understanding of science, rather than needing to develop them as part of the process of learning.

I propose to start with some simple information about, and comparisons of, the statutory orders for English and science, looking at the profile components, Attainment Targets and programmes of study in broad terms. I shall then consider briefly the aspects of the science National Curriculum where teachers of English find a considerable amount of common ground with colleagues in science, and finally address the issues of language and communication, as they relate to students' work in science. I hope to indicate ways in which science teachers and those concerned with supporting students' language development, whether they are specialist English teachers, or experts in teaching English as a second language, or in supporting students with special educational needs, can work together to enable students to learn more effectively in both subject areas.

To start with some simple comparisons of English and science in the National Curriculum:

Profile Components: English 3   (Speaking and Listening;
                                  Reading; Writing)
                      Science 2   (Exploration of . . . ;
                                  Knowledge and Understanding
                                  of . . .)
Attainment Targets: English 5   (AT 1 Speaking and Listening
                                  AT 2 Reading
                                  AT 3, 4, 5 Writing and
                                            Handwriting and
                                            Spelling)
                      Science 17 (the entire Attainment Target)

The English profile components define the subject according to the modes of language activity (talking, reading and writing). The Attainment Targets relate closely to these profile components and define them in terms of process and development. You may find it of interest to compare the way the English profile components are described in their corresponding Attainment Targets with the treatment of the science profile components and Attainment Targets:

Speaking and Listening
English AT 1:   The development of pupils' understanding of the spoken word and the capacity to express themselves effectively in a variety of speaking and listening activities, matching style and response to audience and purpose.

Reading
English AT 2:   The development of the ability to read, understand and respond to all types of writing, as well as the development of information-retrieval strategies for the purposes of study.

Writing
English AT 3:   A growing ability to construct and convey meaning in written language, matching style to audience and purpose.

English AT 4:   Spelling

English AT 5:   Handwriting (at Level 5 and above these become AT 4/5: Presentation).

Of the seventeen science Attainment Targets in the DES (1989) document, only AT1 defines the corresponding profile component in the same way as English does; the remaining sixteen define their relevant profile component in terms of content. Both English and science have to cope with the problems of separating out aspects of a subject which are essentially interrelated. As you can see, the English Attainment Targets set English teachers broad, long-term goals – to enable children to become better and more confident speakers, listeners, readers and writers. In addition the English programmes of study do not specify in detail which books should be read, or which topics should be discussed or written about. They are framed in terms of the opportunities which should be provided in order to enable children to develop and make progress towards meeting the Attainment Targets. Although there are obvious areas, for example literature, personal expression and imaginative writing, where teachers focus attention in English lessons, English as a subject has the advantage of being content free, so that contexts for learning about the processes of becoming a talker, reader and writer are not dictated by the requirement to transmit a body of knowledge. Science teachers, on the other hand, have to balance the demands of a body of content with the need to provide opportunities to learn skills and processes.

Looked at from the point of view of separate subjects, one way in which science and English can meet productively for students is in the provision of these contexts for learning. I am thinking here less of the talk and writing that go on when scientific activities are the focus of their work, and more of the aspects of the science curriculum which are concerned with appreciating the contribution that science makes to society. Discussion of moral and ethical issues form the substance of many English lessons, but can suffer from lack of information so that people express prejudices and notions rather than offering informed arguments. Most discussions could benefit from the emphasis which science places on 'developing students' powers of reasoning' and 'reflecting and thinking about evidence in a disciplined way' (NSG 4.4).

There is also a lot of common ground between science and English teachers in the attitudes which science aims to develop:

- curiosity
- respect for evidence

- willingness to tolerate uncertainty
- critical reflection
- perseverance
- creativity and inventiveness
- open-mindedness
- cooperation with others
- sensitivity to the environment

(NSG 6.6)

What science develops.

English subject

The context where the teaching of English may be said to be most firmly grounded in content is in the study of texts of all kinds. We extend the definition of a text to include literature, ancient and modern, from other cultures as well as from England, fiction, non-fiction, journalism, documentary, autobiography, plays, poems, and visual and media texts. Given the differing contexts the two subject areas provide, the attitudes in the above list (with the possible exception of the last one) are not at all a bad description of what we are also aiming to encourage when we study and discuss texts with students.

However, these are aspects of the science National Curriculum which offer interesting points of contact between the subject areas, but are not necessarily fundamental to matters of pupils' learning in the way that understanding the role of language in their learning is. It is necessary now to make a clear distinction between English as a subject on a timetable and English as the medium of instruction and learning for all the other subjects on that timetable. In other words, to make the distinction between English as a separate subject discipline, and English as what is inadequately termed a 'service' subject to other areas of the curriculum. This is where the points of contact between the English and the science documents seem to me to open up a huge range of possibilities for enhancing students' learning, and where the expertise of colleagues whose work involves supporting students across the curriculum, through ESL or SEN or learning support departments, can be of as much value to science teachers as that of the English specialists.

English teachers would recognize and welcome the following definitions of communication, from the original report of the Science Working Group to the Secretary of State, in which communication was identified as a separate profile component of science:

We see communication as an activity involving both transmission and reception of information, with pupils addressing and responding to a variety of audiences. Central to our view of communication are the notions of range and match. Range in the sense that pupils will . . . make use of a variety of styles, media and devices: talking, listening, writing, drawing, modelling, using texts, journals and newspapers, audio and video recorders, data bases and computer programmes. By match we see pupils varying style and mode of communication to suit audience and purpose. [4.34]
   Communication, in the context of science studies, is active, varied, targeted (to audience and purpose), skill-enhancing and central to effective learning and development. [4.36]

Although it would have been good to see these statements transferred verbatim to the Statutory Orders, it is arguably even more satisfactory from the point of view of students' language development and learning to have communication embedded in the two profile components as it is now, and to have each key stage-related programme of study open with a general introduction which makes explicit what opportunities for communicating their learning students should be offered.

These introductory paragraphs present a steadily expanding view of the ways in which students should be able to report on and respond to what they learn. However, and this brings me at last to the aspects of the science documents which worry me, they seem to take for granted aspects of classroom organization and management, activities and outcomes that English teachers know are complex and that they know need conscious planning, proper resources and sustained support. In its introduction to the original proposals for science, the National Curriculum Council (NCC, 1988) stated:

In developing our attainment targets and programmes of study we have made general assumptions about pupils' capability in areas of English, Welsh (in Welsh speaking schools in Wales) and mathematics. [1.25]

I now propose to address these 'general assumptions', try to indicate the problems which lie behind them, and suggest ways in which teachers might collaborate to address them in the best interests of pupils' learning.

Firstly, the science documents take it for granted that children can:

Can

- read for information
- write notes
- write reports
- present their findings

The programmes of study and statements of attainment seem to assume that children learn content and skills in a sequential and progressive way, moving from content which is small and close to their own interests to topics which are large, distant and increasingly abstract, and from handling limited amounts of material to handling quantity. While there is probably some truth in this, it is instructive to look more closely at the specific language demands made by science AT 1 (Table 3.1), and relate them to the corresponding demands at each notional level of the Attainment Targets for English. In an effort to simplify this exercise, I have tried to isolate the features of the statements of attainment which are directly related to pupils' use of language to learn, and (in the case of Reading and Writing) most directly relevant to science. That is to say language activities which will enable them to:

- understand and clarify their own thinking
- develop powers of reasoning
- reflect and think about evidence
- make ideas available for reflection, discussion and checking

These wordings are taken from the Statutory Orders for English in the National Curriculum (DES and Welsh Office, 1990). Extremely attentive readers of this and *Science: Non-Statutory Guidance* (NCC, 1989), where a similar table appears for levels 1–3, will note differences in wording. Collaborative discussion and interpretation between teachers should now be based on this version.

Apart from demonstrating the absurdity of attempting to define ten possible levels of attainment in talking, reading and writing, drawing attention to the deficiencies of the language when it comes to describing what might possibly happen at the highest levels, and raising impossible questions about assessment, this table might have its uses as a focus for dialogue between science teachers and those concerned with children's language development. I suggest that the most productive way forward might be to ask:

- what would the work described here actually look like?
- what is it reasonable to expect a child or student at this approximate stage to be able to do?

Table 3.1

Science AT 1	Speaking and listening	Reading	Writing
Level 1 Observe Describe Communicate observations	Participate in group activities Respond to simple instructions	Talk in simple terms about information in non-fiction texts	Use pictures, symbols, letters words, phrases to communicate meaning
Level 2 Ask questions Suggest ideas (how, why, what if?) Identify differences List Collate Interpret findings Record findings	Participate in group engaged in given task Talk with teacher, listen, ask and answer questions Give, receive and follow accurately precise instructions when pursuing task individually or in group	Read and understand signs, labels, notices Listen and respond to material read aloud, expressing opinions informed by what has been read	Produce simple coherent non-chronological writing (e.g. lists)
Level 3 Formulate hypotheses Identify and describe simple variables Distinguish between . . . Interpret and generalize Sequence major features of activity	Listen with increasing concentration, responding to questions commenting on what has been said	Devise a clear set of questions that will enable them to select appropriate information sources and reference books from class and school library	Shape writing using range of connectives Produce other types of writing (e.g. notes, plans, diagrams) Begin to revise and redraft

Table 3.1 (*contd*)

Science AT 1	Speaking and listening	Reading	Writing
Level 4			
Plan	Give detailed oral account of something learned in class	Find books or magazines by using classification system	
Follow written instructions		Use appropriate methods of finding information, when pursuing line of enquiry	Produce writing showing evidence of developing ability to structure in ways which make meaning clear (e.g. titles, paragraphs punctuation)
Describe . . . in ordered prose using limited technical vocabulary			
	Explain with reasons why a course of action has been taken		Organize writing for different purposes (e.g. recording something learned) in orderly ways; discuss organization of writing; revise and redraft as appropriate
	Ask and respond to questions in a variety of situations with increasing confidence		
Level 5			
Make written statements of patterns derived from data from various sources	Give well-organized sustained account of . . .		Write in variety of forms for range of purposes and audiences
	Contribute to and respond constructively in discussion	Select reference books and other information materials; use organizational devices to find answers to own questions and those of others	

Table 3.1 (*contd*)

Science AT 1	Speaking and listening	Reading	Writing
	Convey information and ideas effectively in straightforward situation		
	Contribute to planning and participate in group presentation		
Level 6 Contribute to analysis and investigation of collaborative exercise Use experience and knowledge to make predictions . . .		Select from range of reference materials using appropriate methods to identify key points	
Prepare detailed written plan	Contribute considered opinions responsive to contributions of others		
Produce reports which include a critical evaluation of certain features of the experiment . . .	Convey information and ideas effectively in variety of situations where subject is familiar to pupils and audience Contribute to and participate with fluency in group presentation		Write in variety of forms for range of purposes presenting subject matter differently to suit needs of specified known audiences

Table 3.1 (*contd*)

Science AT 1	Speaking and listening	Reading	Writing
Level 7 Plan, design and safely carry out an entire investigation . . . Produce a systematically structured report	Use and understand language which conveys information and ideas effectively when situation or topic is less readily familiar to pupils/audience		Write in wider variety of forms with clear sense of purpose and awareness of audience (e.g. notes, instructions essays, articles. Plan, hypothesize, inform, explain, compare, contrast, persuade . . .)
Accurately use and interpret scientific nomenclature		Select, retrieve, combine information independently from wide range of reference material	
	Take active part in group discussion		
Level 8 Prepare and deliver report matched to audience incorporating background material from variety of sources	Convey information and ideas in variety of complex situations involving range of audiences, in language matched to context and purpose		Write in wide variety of forms, with clear sense of purpose, demonstrating ability to judge appropriate length and form for given task
		Select, retrieve, evaluate and combine information independently from comprehensive range of reference material	

Table 3.1 (*contd*)

Science AT 1	Speaking and listening	Reading	Writing
Level 9 Literature search (as part of range of exploratory techniques)	Give presentation on complex subject cogently and clearly, integrating talk with writing and other media where appropriate	As Level 8, making effective use of the material	Organize and present subject matter appropriately for specified audiences known and unknown
Level 10	Take a variety of leading roles in group discussion, listening with understanding and noting salient points	As Levels 8 and 9, but also making effective and sustained use of material	Organize complex, demanding or extended subject matter clearly and effectively; produce well-structured pieces of writing . . . use wide range of vocabulary

- how could we make it possible for a child or student to perform these tasks?
- what additional resources and/or support might be necessary?

It is a formidable collection of language demands, but one in which an English teacher can see enormous potential, as well as enormous difficulties. Children are not born with the ability to perform any of these language activities, but they can learn to do them if they are given appropriate opportunities, and also shown how. Separating the list into levels is helpful in one way, in that it indicates some sort of notion of the nature and depth of the activity which would be taking place when these different abilities could be demonstrated. But in another way, it is not helpful at all. Language development is not a sequential and linear process; separating the activities according to levels may give the illusion that it would be possible to cross-reference students' activities between English and science and ensure that if they need to be able to 'describe in ordered prose' or 'select and weigh evidence in order to form reasoned judgments', they can be shown how to do it in English and then transfer that knowledge and skill to science without difficulty. As we all know from our own experience, it doesn't work quite as simply as that!

This is the reason why it is so good to see the science documents refer so often to the importance of the context within which learning science is taking place. All the elements of this context – the subject label on the timetable, the surroundings in which lessons take place, the focus of attention, the behaviour expected, the kinds of question asked, the answers acknowledged, and also the types of response and recording, written or graphic, which are expected – can offer a supportive framework within which learning to think, talk, read and write like a scientist can take place, provided that it is not taken for granted that students can use the language of science 'naturally'. The science documents also emphasize the importance of talk and classroom interaction as part of communicating and developing scientific understanding. As well as being important in its own right, talk is a vital precursor to writing when concepts are being internalized and ideas are being explored. Learning the language of any subject, being able to manipulate it and make it say what you want it to, takes time and practice. It is not just a matter of learning new vocabulary and how to spell it; it also involves learning appropriate forms and structures and conventions of style. It might be helpful for science teachers to consider the significant differences for them between spoken and written language, which should help them find ways of helping students to write science more successfully. Learning to write in a subject often takes place in much the same way as learning to talk – by copying those around you, and learning by experience. Learning to write science could be made easier for pupils if they were given plenty of good models of how to do it. This would involve making available to them well-written, accessible materials about science in books, magazines and newspapers, as well as showing students how to write up an experiment or organize a report. This is not advocating a return to the use of rigid formulas for carrying out these tasks, but is an acknowledgement of the support that people need in order to become successful communicators, particularly in writing.

When considering the kinds of talk and writing that pupils

undertake in science, teachers might find it useful to ask themselves a few basic questions. *Science: Non-Statutory Guidance* (7.10) offers a helpful checklist for selecting and evaluating particular learning experiences. To this could be added:

OPPORTUNITIES FOR SPEAKING AND LISTENING:

- is talk (in this lesson) the appropriate means of learning (compared with listening, reading and writing)?
- is it the starting point, from which other activities will develop?
- is it to be used to demonstrate learning?

In other words, is it the medium for the learning, or the starting point or a significant part of the final outcome? Related to this would be similar questions about the groupings in which pupils will work, and the ways these relate to the role of talk in the lesson:

- will this be a whole-class discussion — if so will it really involve the whole class, or just one or two pupils?
- will girls and boys speak, or just boys?
- will it be pupil talk or teacher talk?
- how much time will they spend in pairs/small groups?
- how will presentations and feedback be organized?

As well as recognizing the importance of talk, the science documents also emphasize the importance of a sense of purpose and audience as part of effective communication (NCC, 1989, 9.0 and AT 1 L8; General Introduction to the Programmes of Study for each Key Stage). Purpose and audience are key concepts for English teachers; we recognize them as factors which have a major effect on the ways in which people speak and write. In developing a student's ability to communicate effectively it is essential to help them to understand that there is an audience for what they have to say, and to realize the implications of this fact for the ways they talk and write. The audience may be, as the science documents suggest, other children, teachers, parents and other adults. For certain kinds of writing it may be the student him or herself. Teachers need to be aware of the range of potential audiences, provide real ones where possible and relevant, and be clear in their own minds about the kinds of writing which are appropriate in different situations.

Science teachers might find it useful to consider the following questions in relation to specific pieces of writing done by their pupils:

   1. Purpose: what is this piece of writing for?

- to record what happened?
- to organize the pupil's thinking?
- to clarify the pupil's ideas?

What difference might/would it make to the quality of the communication here if the pupil had had a genuine need to convey information/ideas to someone else?

   2. Audience: who is the audience for this piece of writing?
What difference would it make to the way in which pupils have written if the audience were clearly identified for them as:

- themselves?
- their peers—who were part of the activity written about?
- their peers—who were *not* part of the activity written about?
- the teacher—who was the initiator of the activity?
  - —who was *not* the initiator, but was present throughout the activity?
- an examiner, who is unknown to the writer?
- unspecified?

Such questions might prove helpful in distinguishing between the kinds of writing being asked for and produced, and also in differentiating between pieces of writing produced by different pupils for the same purpose, in terms of how successfully each writer has managed to carry out what she or he set out to do.

The other major unexamined assumption in the science Attainment Targets is that pupils can use secondary sources to complement their learning in science.

Points 1 and 2 above isolate the reading-for-information element of the English Reading profile component. It is something about which many English teachers feel ambivalent and guilty, I think. On the one hand, we want children to read widely—we lament the fact that boys in particular seem to give up reading fiction at quite an early age; we put a lot of emphasis on reading for pleasure, and then equate that with reading novels, which it may be for girls, but obviously isn't so much for boys. The reasons for this are complex, but the results are that while girls become increasingly skilled readers of narrative, boys' preferences for factual information enable them to develop skills in reading information texts, which girls may continue to find difficult. The conventions of an informa- tion text — layout, relationship of print to pictures, use of diagrams, sentence structures and language forms — are alien to many readers and we do little to correct this by consciously helping all students to learn how such texts 'work'. Academic texts, including school text- books, can present particular problems to inexperienced readers, who may be struggling simultaneously with difficult ideas expressed in unfamiliar language. Despite these difficulties, research done by the Effective Use of Reading project (Lunzer and Gardner, 1979) showed that although science texts were often the hardest to read because of their subject-specific vocabulary and language structures, most reading that was done 'for science' was done unsupported — a chapter of a textbook for homework, or as the result of a general instruction to 'find out about' something related to the topic of a lesson. The method advocated in the science National Curriculum documents, of presenting children with a limited number of secondary sources at first, and gradually expand- ing the range of materials from which they are supposed to draw their information, seems logical, but does not address the problem of how readers find their way about in and use the texts they read. The answer is not always to reduce the reading demands which the subject makes, by resorting to worksheets, or doing the sum- marizing for them. We are all familiar with the 'project' which is no more than copying out, and shows little understanding of the texts which have been used, and little ability to make the ideas the student's own. Teachers need to think of ways of supporting students in their reading, by giving them an indication of the way the content of the chapter is structured, or by posing key questions which can be answered by the reading. There is an important area for collaboration between science and English teachers here, in con- sidering the readability levels of texts, finding supportive ways of encouraging the reading of them and teaching children the skills of research and reading for information. There is no reason why science teachers should have to cope with this on their own; on the other hand, no amount of study skills teaching or library skills delivered outside a subject-specific context will actually enable chil- dren to use secondary sources with confidence and appropriateness.

Similar problems also need to be aired in relation to the use of film and video. If the overall aim of the curriculum is to enable students to be able to form their own judgements about what they read and see, and to be able to express informed opinions, then they need the skills to 'read' a visual text just as much as they need the skills to read print. While many of the visual resources used in science may be ideologically impartial, the same cannot be said of what students see or read on television or in the press. AT 17 — the nature of science — would seem to offer ideal opportunities for collaboration between teachers of science and English or media studies, perhaps as part of students' wider science and media education.

I have left until last two major areas: assessment and possibilities for cross-curricular collaboration of various kinds. For both science and English teachers the issues related to the assessment of their subjects loom large, and I am uncertain to what extent it is justifiable to encourage people to see assessment as another cross-curricular activity. Arrangements to share in the assessment of students' performance in aspects of either subject are probably better left to individuals to organize for themselves in their own institutional contexts. However, there are some general points which it is worth raising here.

Since English aims to assess students' abilities in the four modes of language across a wide variety of activities, there are certain aspects of their achievement in English in the National Curriculum which may well be better demonstrated in other subject contexts than they can be in English lessons. Reading for information is one of the most obvious of these; the other is aspects of speaking and listening. In both cases what their English teacher will need is a record of what the student has done over a period of time, rather than a judgement on the level of performance at any one moment in time. Many students are used to keeping logs or journals of their work in various aspects of English, particularly those which involve much group and collaborative work towards a final product. It would be extremely useful to both English and science teachers to have a record of the reading done in the context of science, and also of participation in group discussions and presentations. Since one of the aims of both subjects is to encourage students to reflect more consciously on their learning, it might be more productive for these records to be kept by the students themselves, rather than adding another task to their teacher's workload. What it would require from the science teacher is commitment to its usefulness, willingness to allocate some class time on a regular basis to filling the record in, and willingness to spend some time, again on a reasonably regular basis, with the appropriate colleague teaching English to talk about their perceptions of the student's strengths and weaknesses as a talker and a reader. This suggestion clearly has implications for whole-school recording and reporting policies and schedules, and for the ways in which students opt for or are allocated to groups for science and English.

Science: Non-Statutory Guidance suggests that a second stage of curriculum planning, after defining the scientific aspects of an activity, should be to consider the 'opportunities for the use and development of English' which it offers. I have suggested some questions that science teachers might consider when planning activities which necessarily involve talk and writing, as part of the process and as outcomes. It would also be possible, where circumstances are favourable, to plan certain units of work, where, for example, the planning and delivery of presentations to report on scientific activities might be done in English time. Such a situation, in which the English teacher would be providing a real audience for the presentations, and would be perceived by the students to be asking 'real' questions, would provide good opportunities to assess aspects of speaking and listening which might otherwise go unrewarded. Appropriate methods would, of course, have to be devised to assess the knowledge and understanding of the science demonstrated.

It remains to try to suggest ways forward for collaboration between science and English teachers in planning for and implementing the National Curriculum. There seem to me to be a number of possibilities, of different kinds. For me the most important and potentially productive is between department and department, teacher and teacher, working towards shared understandings of the aims of each subject and the demands they make on students, particularly as users of language. Any dialogue which enables English teachers to form a clearer understanding of what it is that students need to be able to do with language in order to be successful in science, and which enables science teachers to understand more fully the part they can play in supporting students' language development will have beneficial effects on teaching and learning.

Another way of collaborating is through shared content, perhaps organized through topics or themes. While much excellent cross-curricular work in primary schools arises out of science content, this seems harder to manage within the subject-defined timetables of secondary schools. What it requires is teams of teachers committed to planning and working together, enabled by timetabling arrangements that allow for this collaboration to happen properly. Failing that, collaboration at teacher level again might throw up ways in which English teachers could support and reinforce work in science — by reading biographies and stories of relevant scientists, for example, or synchronizing a study of Brecht's *Galileo* with the appropriate unit of key stage 3 science. The non-statutory guidance also suggests interesting possibilities of links with drama and history. My own view is that any attempts to coordinate content should be judged by the criteria of coherence for the students, and not become a mix 'n' match exercise at teacher level about notions around relevant bits of knowledge and content. Better, I think, for most of us to leave content to the scientists, and work on the cross-curricular applications of the modes of language, while enabling people who are interested to experiment on a manageable scale with different kinds of cross-curricular collaboration.

In conclusion, I would just remind colleagues who teach science that the relationship between science and English has been long and productive. The research team working on the Schools Council Writing across the Curriculum project, who published *Writing and Learning across the Curriculum 11–16* (Martin *et al.*, 1976), found more interest in their work from science teachers than from any other group except English teachers. The development of Nuffield science and the work done on science as process bear witness to a shared concern about how people learn as much as about what they learn. I think it is important for us to see the National Curriculum as a way for teachers to work together across the boundaries of their subjects, and as another chapter in the story of those who are interested in how children learn, and how teachers can help them to do it more effectively.

REFERENCES

DES [Department of Education and Science] and the Welsh Office (1989) *Science in the National Curriculum*. London: HMSO (March).
DES [Department of Education and Science] and the Welsh Office (1990) *English in the National Curriculum (No. 2)*. London: HMSO.

Lunzer, E. and Gardner, K. (eds) (1979) *The Effective Use of Reading*. London: Heinemann Education.

Martin, N., d'Arcy, P., Newton, B. and Parker, R. (1976) *Writing and Learning across the Curriculum 11-16*. London: Ward Lock Educational.

NCC [National Curriculum Council] (1988) *Science for Ages 5 to 16*. Proposals of the Secretary of State for Education. London: DES and Welsh Office.

NCC [National Curriculum Council] (1989) *Science: Non-Statutory Guidance*. York: National Curriculum Council (June).

Chapter 4

Science and Technology

Alan West

THE PLACE OF SCIENCE IN TECHNOLOGY: THE PLACE OF TECHNOLOGY IN SCIENCE?

It is the autumn term in an inner-city, single-sex secondary school in Birmingham. The girls assemble outside the art room for their timetabled double lesson of art, carrying the usual schoolbags and in addition, on this occasion, a collection of plastic carrier bags — most of them bulging, some with leaves and stalks protruding. Besides the usual talk of the weekend exploits and the last television episode of 'Neighbours' there is a general buzz of comparison — centred on the contents of the plastic carrier bags!

As the students (Year 8) move into the room, they disperse into small groups and prepare for the task in hand: the production of handmade paper from a range of available vegetable and recyclable materials. To reach this point they had been working on a theme for the term concerned with paper and paper making. Their art teacher had introduced them to traditional paper-making techniques based on his own out-of-school interests, and as a consequence of media reports at the time concerned with the 'problems' anticipated as a consequence of the relatively rapid deterioration and ageing of mass-produced paper. The girls had identified a variety of needs arising from the stimulus of 'wanting to know why modern paper didn't last as long as paper made by traditional methods': clearly this *was* the case since their experience of seeing old books, paper prints and sketches in museums was at variance with the kind of deterioration and discolouring they had observed for newsprint and paperback books. They wanted to produce long-lasting paper for their own art work and they saw advantage in moving away from mass-produced to handmade material which, because of its crafted nature, had greater aesthetic visual appeal.

As the lesson progressed the various interest-based project teams set about their problem-solving tasks. In attempting to make 'interesting paper' they had brought a variety of what they hoped would be suitable vegetable matter to use as a starting point. The range extended from nettles to maize, lettuce to dock leaves. They were free to experiment with conditions such as:

- the extent to which the raw fibre was chopped
- the time the fibre was steeped in sodium hydroxide solution
- the temperature at which the process took place
- the effects of final pulp pH and pH correction

Some of the teams were involved in designing and making the equipment required for the process. As the school term slipped by, sheets of paper were produced on the paper-making frames the students had constructed. The quality and 'fitness for purpose' of the sheets were investigated. The students were keen to compare the physical properties of the product (such as strength and absorbency) as well as considering the aesthetic appeal of the material for artistic purposes. They were also prompted to think about the marketability of their handmade sheet paper as a result of the considerable interest generated by visitors to the school. It appeared they had produced a much sought-after commodity!

The girls had negotiated their problem-solving activity with teachers and 'adults other than teachers' (AOTs) in the classroom, using the CREST (Creativity in Science and Technology) award scheme profile. The adults were industrialists and people from the local polytechnic who were interested in the project.

BUT WAS IT ART, SCIENCE OR TECHNOLOGY?

Although this experience predated the National Curriculum, in many ways it pre-empted the type of work currently envisaged within the National Curriculum technology document (DES, 1990). And in the project's conception and delivery, it certainly provided opportunities to explore issues relevant to the present curriculum debate and state of development.

Aspects of the National Curriculum technology document will touch every teacher of science (and, of course, many other teachers besides). In this chapter I want to focus on the key issues arising from this document as they impinge on the work of science teachers. Such issues range across a spectrum extending from individual science teachers' perceptions of the document, to departmental and whole-school issues. I hope readers will bear with me if I draw extensively on examples from the CREST project which, not unnaturally, I feel can make an interesting contribution to the way technology is developed in schools. I will describe the project more fully later.

First, I want to consider the way in which the 'technological process', developed through the technology programmes of study, can — in part — both be realized *through* the context of science and also be seen to *enrich* that context.

Secondly, I want to explore a particular view of technology education. This is a multi-faceted view and I will focus on one principal feature — the building of cross-curricular problem-solving teams.

Throughout the chapter I want to identify issues that will enable science teachers to liaise and build links with other areas of school life, all of which are directly and indirectly influenced by the technology document. Finally, I try to summarize the discussion with a 'to do' list based on my key issues.

But now to avoid answering the question 'What is technology?' There are probably as many definitions as there are technologists and scientists and this chapter is not long enough to do justice to the question. In the end, in schools we have to work with that which the powers that be have provided for us. The National Curriculum Council's non-statutory guidelines (NCC, 1990) say:

> Design and technology is an activity which spans the curriculum, drawing on and linking a range of subjects. By creating a new subject area, work at present undertaken in art and design, business education, craft design and technology, home economics and information technology will be coordinated to improve pupils' understanding of the significance of technology to the economy and the quality of life. . . . [It] describes a way of working in which pupils investigate a need or respond to an opportunity to make or modify something. They use their knowledge and understanding to devise a method or

solution, realise it practically and evaluate the end product and decisions taken during the process.

So technology is not a remix of traditional subject areas, it is to be a new subject. It is concerned with developing technological capability in a practical, applied way and in this respect may be seen to be drawing on knowledge and understanding from a number of subject areas, including science. The statutory orders for technology identify two profile components:

- design and technology capability
- information technology capability

Design and technology (D&T) capability, they say, is about 'identifying needs, generating ideas, making and testing to find the best solutions'. Information technology capability (IT), on the other hand, has been identified by the NCC as a cross-curricular skill and as such should be taught as 'an integral part of most foundation subjects': 'Information Technology is concerned with storing, processing and presenting information by electronic means.' Again, the emphasis is on practical capability in that students must be presented with the opportunity to use IT as a routine part of their school work, and in so doing become better prepared to transfer this confidence into working life. In this respect the opportunity to use IT in a range of contexts is seen as a part of a student's minimum educational entitlement.

In common with the technology document, it is convenient to consider these two capabilities separately. As there is space here to discuss only one, I have chosen design and technology capability. I am trading on the fact that IT capability is to appear through all subject areas and so will be dealt with elsewhere.

D&T CAPABILITY – THE NCC VERSION

In the document, D&T capability is profile component 1. In addition to what I have already quoted, the document continues by describing 'pupil enterprise'. This, they say, is the ability

> to work as members of a team, contribute to their success in design and technology. As their experience grows they will understand that technological development rarely ends, since the evaluation of a

product offers new opportunities for improvement. Pupils will be able to work to deadlines, keep to budgets and reconcile conflicting requirements such as quality, speed and cost. They will acquire a range of skills and work with a variety of materials. This process is described as design and technology capability . . . [and also involves] . . .

- deciding what is worth doing and achievable
- generating and appraising possible solutions
- reconciling conflicting demands
- making decisions on the basis of imperfect information
- achieving outcomes within constraints of time and cost

Within this, inside PC 1, there are four Attainment Targets which can be summarized as follows: AT 1 — identifying needs and opportunities; AT 2 — generating a design; AT 3 — planning and making; AT 4 — evaluating.

Putting the science non-statutory guidelines (NCC, 1989) alongside technology allows me to draw out some of the parallels. These are the words from science:

> 5.1   Technology is a creative human activity which brings about desired changes by making, controlling or improving the way in which things work through design and by using relevant knowledge and resources.

> 5.2   Scientific and Design and Technology classroom activity may be difficult to distinguish. Indeed, some teachers have been introduced to Design and Technology through practical science and vice versa.

However, it is wise to draw out some important differences in style and purpose between the two: science is *not* technology and cannot therefore be seen as synonymous with it. Science is enquiry-led and concerned with the pursuit of better investigative strategies, more reliable knowledge about the physical and biological world. Design and technology, by the above definition, is led by the desire to meet human needs and opportunities. Clearly, there are important connections between the two. For example, science draws on design and technology in developing instrumentation and techniques of enquiry; significant discoveries have been dependent upon the development of particular tools, materials or techniques.

The technology document describes five contexts for pupil activities based on home, school and recreation, community, business, and industry, though students may work in other contexts at any of the key stages. For AT 1, the Attainment Level statements for D&T involve such things as:

- describing to others what has been noticed
- suggesting practical changes that could be made in response to a need
- using their knowledge and the results of investigations to identify needs
- opportunities for D&T activities to move progressively from familiar to unfamiliar situations
- the students should: provide oral and written justification for the conclusions they reach as a result of investigation
- vary methods of investigation to obtain all the information required
- plan in detail the various stages of their investigation

The spirit, if not the actual words, will be familiar to all science teachers from the science document. Clearly, acts of questioning, describing, planning, changing, selecting and modifying are areas common to both curricula. In turn, AT 2 is concerned with producing a design proposal and developing it into a realistic design. The realism may be based, for example, in knowledge and understanding of some aspect of science. A sample of level statements reveals that students have to:

- apply knowledge and skills to select ideas for different parts of a design
- record ideas as they develop
- estimate the resource requirements and check on availability
- make judgements about realistic ways forward by exploring alternative solutions and use these to refine their design proposal
- plan activities to take into account multiple constraints which may at times be conflicting

Briefly, AT 3 is concerned with planning and making, to include:

- using knowledge of materials and equipment in making artefacts, systems or environments
- working with others in planning and apportioning tasks
- using knowledge of technical and symbolic representations of materials and components and processes to assist making

Finally, AT 4 is concerned with evaluating the processes, products and effects of pupils' activities; pupils evaluate their own work and that of others to:

- describe to others what they have done
- discuss with others to justify the ideas, materials, components, procedures, techniques and processes used, and indicate possible improvements
- devise and carry out ways of testing the extent to which a product satisfies their design specification
- illustrate the economic, moral, social and environmental consequences of design

These last two targets can be seen to have parallels in science in the conduct of investigations, use of apparatus for measurement and observation. Here again there are opportunities to develop a consistent set of student experiences. Interpreting and communicating ideas and results are key areas in science. Evaluating outcomes, their validity, and the design, preparation and delivery of reports geared to a particular audience are directly linked to levels of attainment in science.

THE NEW VISION

Let me reinforce once again that D&T capability is not exclusively the domain of the traditional CDT areas within schools. During the 1990 SCSST (Standing Conference on Schools' Science and Technology) annual conference, Paul Black, in his keynote address, made the following point about the key features of the new technology curriculum:

> the first of these features is that we must accept a new vision. The subject is radically new and unless those involved see it as radically new, they might be missing the point. That is, anyone who says 'we are doing this already, we already handle this in business studies very well, or in CDT very well, and it only needs a minor adaption' will probably be missing the point — of range and quality of aims and experiences.
>
> (Black, 1990)

The aims and experiences he refers to were concerned with practical capability. The comments made during this address may be seen to be building on his frequently quoted paper 'In place of confusion'

(Black and Harrison, 1985). The key issues here are: what are the main features of this new vision, and can science — and technology — make the vision real? I have chosen, so far, to look closely at technological capability as it is perceived within the technology document and the way in which this maps on to the process skills of science developed through investigation in AT 1.

But let me take this further. I want to use a checklist which I consider to be useful as a backdrop to just a part of my interpretation of the new vision. The checklist forms a substantial part of a 'purpose statement' designed to support an in-service education programme. In this programme, teachers were placed in a situation where they experienced directly how industry-related problem solving (such as that stimulated by CREST) might be used to help deliver cross-curricular technology. They were encouraged to see how well this experience applies to pupils who are to acquire technological capability through the National Curriculum's programmes of study.

In my view, students' problem-solving experiences should take place in a way which:

- fosters partnership
- focuses on the needs of schools, students, teachers and industrialists
- develops interpersonal skills
- develops the concept of an effective team
- highlights the process of learning from experience
- identifies strategies and models for using profiling activities such as CREST in the cross-curricular delivery of technology
- offers an identifiable path forward in terms of progression for students
- is enjoyable

It is immensely difficult to separate some of these issues — particularly since in the CREST project they are *not* separate but slip easily from one point of concern to another. Therefore it is easier to begin by discussing the 'fostering of partnerships' and make reference to the other features on the list as they occur. The particular partnerships I have in mind are teams, and their ways of working to facilitate technology entitlement for students.

Partnership issues are particularly important as problem solving develops in the five contexts (home, school and recreation, community, business, and industry) and the last one, industry, is ideal for linking to real-life problems. Facilitating effective partnerships is essential on a number of levels:

pupil : pupil
pupil : teacher
teacher : teacher
pupil : AOT
teacher : AOT

In both science and D&T, emphasis is placed on the ability of students to work collaboratively on project work and to be part of a team. The technology Attainment Targets (at the higher levels) recognize project and team leadership as an important skill and one which provides differentiation between level statements. Providing students with the opportunity to work in this way, particularly when the project work is extended over a 30-hour period as recommended at technology key stage 4 (KS 4), presents teachers with an organizational challenge with common elements in both science and technology.

Let's take an example. At a recent Surrey Science and Technology Regional Organization (SATRO) summer school a group of youngsters came together from different forms within the same school to tackle a problem: to design a modular system for producing special television effects. This was to use blue-background colour picture separation technology. In a nutshell, they had to produce a system that allowed two TV pictures to be superimposed without the two moving relative to each other as the cameras were moved. The problem was introduced by an 'industrial partner' and the team had to gel quickly to break the problem into linked parts so that each component could be designed by subsets of the team in such a way that, at the end of the day, the whole was equal to (or better than) the sum of the parts. They also had to be mindful of the way in which they were to report on their activities to a plenary session at the end of the time. In their case they took the 'proof of the pudding' option and produced a short video that demonstrated the effects they wanted. What fostered partnership here? First, the leadership role changed as the project developed. In this case the change evolved with time but was also prompted by the industrial partner asking the team to reflect on their working process as each day's work proceeded. But each day someone emerged to lead the group, coordinate actions and push on to the next stage of the project. Secondly, other roles were adopted and changed, too. So there were 'doers', 'thinkers', 'equipment managers', 'leaders' and so on. The coming together of the component parts had to be coordinated, and the group needed continually to foster different partnerships as the tasks changed and came to fruition. All along, the industrialist had a changing relationship with the team, from 'uncle' to partner, teacher to friend, co-worker to evaluator.

This leads me to the methods selected by the students to report their work, which can be particularly important in ensuring that progression is maintained within the project team — by all of the members. Identifying an individual's contribution to a group effort is frequently an area of anxiety for teachers and this is an issue worthy of discussion. In my example, the whole team took the praise for the project although it was recognized that two in particular were the driving force behind the ideas. Ideally, assessments of team tasks would be undertaken by a group of colleagues drawn from across the school, rather than exclusively from science and technology. In many cases teachers have found the CREST profile particularly useful in monitoring an individual student's progress within a group project. This has been designed to support problem-solving activities and requires students themselves to provide evidence that certain skills are met through the project. As an open document the profile provides a starting point for negotiation between students and teachers (or AOTs) who are in a position to discuss this evidence.

This type of documentation is particularly useful when project work is taking place between a number of working centres within a school. For another example, Year 7 students at a Wirral school have addressed the theme of 'improving the quality of life of an old or infirm person'. They were free to organize their project work between a number of science and technology 'working spaces' within the school, depending on the project's stage of development and the need for specialist services, equipment or materials. Here, the profile provided a readily transferable documentation of skills between one area and another and between teachers working in different areas. It is interesting to note that negotiation over a project profile (and the evidence) provides quite a different experience in working with students, one in which the 'facilitator role' becomes much more significant than the role of 'information provider'.

Clearly in situations like this, where large numbers of students are block-timetabled across CDT, textiles, home economics and science, the staff must share a common perception of the learning outcomes they anticipate will derive from the students' experiences, and — arguably — for this to happen they must also share a perception of science and technology capability.

But teams do not have to be *just* pupil orientated; teacher–teacher teams are profitable too.

TEACHER–TEACHER TEAMS

The statutory guidance for technology (DES, 1990) identifies the key areas within a school for delivering profile component 1 as:

craft
design and technology
home economics
textiles

However, whereas these are key areas, they are not the only areas where technology teaching takes place.

The vision of a 'new' technology may cross these curriculum areas — or cross any extended group of teachers within a school. Black's notion that departments will say 'we are already doing this' painfully highlights the situation likely to be found in some schools. It is important, though, that the cross-curricular basis of the technology Attainment Targets be given a chance to surface and it is imperative that scientists are part of the team involved. A key management issue for all involved is to ensure that the teams responsible for its delivery have a shared vision of technology. To labour the point: technology is not just a part of CDT or of physics, but must be seen as a capability which can be realized across a range of activities. I see the building of cross-curricular technology teams as a key development issue for schools addressing the spirit of 'new' technology. It was probably a key issue for the 'old technology' too but we now have a major chance to put ideals into practice. This is particularly the case where colleagues in traditional departments — indeed within a whole school — may need to reform their perceptions of the curriculum contribution their subject can make. The 'technology team' is an important issue since some teachers in the group will feel disenfranchised by the newness of the 'new technology' and its implications for existing subject content and methodology.

It is my recent experience that such team building can be achieved very effectively by bringing together teachers to solve problems at their own level rather than at the level of their students (West and Watts, 1990). This model provides an excellent way of involving industrial partners with teacher teams so that short- and long-term benefits are derived for all.

Science teachers are often in a very good position to initiate such activities. On a recent occasion, for instance, teachers contributing to the technology programme of their school were invited to work together on a problem identified by a local plastics company which involved the participation of their scientists and engineers as team members. The teachers were in a position to analyse the contributions to 'capability in technology' being made across the group and, in some instances, to 'really talk' to each other for the first time. They were able to value each other's contributions and had the opportunity to reflect on school organization and management — an important feature of the process. By the way, they evaluated the development of their own technological capability by using a CREST profile.

TECHNOLOGY CAN BE ENJOYABLE

The last feature of the 'new technology' stands out in my list. In the examples I have offered so far there is no doubt that cross-curricular problem solving can be highly motivating and enjoyable. One more example. Here the group's (KS 4) brief was to 'design a milk-based dessert suitable for (and enjoyed by) physically handicapped children'.

One can see immediately that this calls on worries about texture (it had to stick to the spoon — but not in the throat!), nutritional requirements, taste, visual appeal, packaging, labelling, and so on. Again, the final 'proof of the pudding' was the product's acceptability to the customers: other pupils at a local school for handicapped children. The process of sampling, colouring, tasting, trialling textures — and working with the clients and end-users — was immensely enjoyable. The final accolade (and summative judgement) came from one youngster who was not normally inclined to use a spoon. In this instance, the chocolate pudding variety was such a success that the contents were demolished and bowl licked clean — the product, it was said, was finger-lickin' good!

Needless to say, sustaining large numbers of student-initiated and student-owned projects presents a significant organizational challenge to any teacher. An effective partnership, which involves outside agencies and support, can do much to offset what at first might appear a daunting prospect.

CREST

The acronym CREST stands for CREativity in Science and Technology and represents a scheme sponsored by the Department of Education and Science and industry, and supported jointly by the British Association for the Advancement of Science (BA) and the Standing Conference on Schools Science and Technology (SCSST). It is coordinated at a local level through science and technology regional organizations and by some local education authorities. The entire project is basically an award scheme for rewarding youngsters' efforts in school; the project's primary aim is to promote scientific and technological problem solving in the 11 to 18 age range. In this sense, it builds on the Young Investigators scheme, also sponsored by the BA, which is targeted at the junior school age range, 8–11. Both schemes aim to complement normal school work and are non-competitive: youngsters gain recognition for their work through the scheme as a national project, and receive a bronze, silver or gold award. CREST awards are criterion referenced, and are designed to stimulate and support problem-solving activity. The scheme encourages, in its early phases, and requires (in its latter phases) students to identify and work on their own problems. These problems are identified through an 'active partnership' between the students or school, and the industrial/business community.

How, you might ask, can students be encouraged to identify their own problems? Much depends on the freedom to choose, and the flexibility of schools (and adaptability of teachers) in allowing students to pursue an investigative pathway — within limits.

CREST places considerable emphasis on 'problem identification', 'negotiation' and links between the student or schools and a range of outside agencies. Students are encouraged to develop their own strategies and (within the safety of the laboratory or workshop) are allowed to experience the successes (and failures) associated with project management. Negotiation at regular intervals over the criteria provides powerful insight for the students. They are not told what to do but are helped to achieve what they want in pursuit of their project objectives. The quality of the students' experiences is monitored using the profile, which asks for the evidence they consider demonstrates the CREST process criteria. A series of 'You Can' statements on a record card maintained by both students and teachers points the way towards iterative problem-solving and successful project completion.

The three stages of the CREST award are addressed by an accumulating set of criteria – a ladder of achievement in problem-solving process skills.

A major point of CREST is that youngsters work on their own project. Individually or in groups, the project is one that they choose. Teachers may be influential at the point of choice, as may the CREST local organizer, but the emphasis is heavily weighted towards the youngster designing his or her own investigation. At the end, students are required to explain the development and outcomes of their projects to the outside agencies who have supported their work. The scheme works equally well for both teams and individual student effort. This is particularly so at the level of silver and gold, where the scheme is looking for quite original (creative) work.

One of CREST's secondary aims is to promote closer working relationships between schools and industry and commerce in the outside world. Some projects have involved the electronics industry; for example, youngsters have designed a '7-day pet-cat feeding system' so that the cat's owners can leave the pet well fed while they are on holiday; or a system for allowing only the owner's cat through the cat flap.

Link organizations like SATROs exist to facilitate the formation of such local partnerships. Practical help for schools might also appear in the form of neighbourhood engineers (volunteer expert help available for projects) organized through the Engineering Council, or electrical engineers organized through the Institute of Electrical Engineers through their project UNCLE. The CREST scheme also offers AOT support through local partnerships organized by the SATRO network.

The effective use of such AOT support for project work must be negotiated. Team working on real problems supported by teachers and AOTs provides an excellent vehicle for students to explore the use of their science knowledge and investigative and process skills within a technological context.

My final example concerns two students whose work was facilitated through a chemical industry link. The students were provided with access to the company's library and to pilot plant facilities. During a visit to the research laboratories the students became aware of the traditional techniques in use to determine the quality of fat used for soap making, techniques which were highly empirical. The two identified a link between their work at school and the updating of the technology used for determining fat quality. Their idea was to build a computer-linked calorimeter capable of operating at saponification temperatures, to analyse the reaction of any fat with sodium hydroxide, and to provide some idea of the suitability of the fat. The students became involved in the technology of calorimeter design and the electronics of high-temperature probes which could be interfaced to a BBC computer. With apparatus developed, they undertook detailed data-logging activities on a series of fats used by the company to make soap. The computer software, written by the students, compared experimental with theoretical temperature changes for reactions involving the fats — with the eventual outcome that a plant operator might be provided with a clear indication of the conversion rate of the fat to soap in the manufacturing process and be able to adjust conditions accordingly.

Throughout the development of the project the students were in regular contact with company staff, who were able to review and evaluate the project on a regular basis. The final outcome was a usable system and tangible recognition of the students' efforts with a CREST award, presented at a national ceremony.

The new vision of technology, and of science, requires that students undertake relevant activity as a vehicle for developing knowledge, understanding and appropriate practical skills and capabilities. Within this chapter I have suggested that links with outside agencies can facilitate such a teaching and learning strategy. Moreover, developing cross-curricular technology teams can do much to increase the opportunity for teachers to explore together the issues of technological capability in a way which is both beneficial to their own professional development and increases the opportunity for their students to realize their scientific and technological entitlement.

Partnership activity is at the core of this area of curriculum development, and a range of external agencies exist to foster and support links. Why not take the opportunity to share the new vision through the type of active learning described?

REFERENCES

Black, P. (1990) *Implementing Technology in the National Curriculum*. Mimeograph, King's College, London. A keynote address to the SCSST Annual Conference, London.

Black, P. and Harrison, G. (1985) *In Place of Confusion*. London: Nuffield/Chelsea Curriculum Trust; Nottingham: Trent Polytechnic.

DES [Department of Education and Science] (1989) *Science in the National Curriculum*. London: HMSO.

DES [Department of Education and Science] (1990) *Technology in the National Curriculum*. London: HMSO.

NCC [National Curriculum Council] (1989) *Science: Non-Statutory Guidance*. London: HMSO.

NCC [National Curriculum Council] (1990) *Technology: Non-Statutory Guidance*. London: HMSO.

West, A. and Watts, D. M. (1990) *Working towards Environmental Enterprise: Issues from a Problem-solving Weekend*. Mimeograph, Educational Liaison Centre, University of Surrey.

Chapter 5

Science and the Humanities

Gwyn Edwards

> surely we have reached the point in the development of educational
> goals of seeing the necessity for both humanistic and scientific under-
> standing in every person, and the way in which these understandings
> overlap and even sometimes integrate.
>
> (Jarrett, 1973)

As the title and above quote suggest, this chapter will endeavour to
identify and examine some of the key issues emanating from the
implementation of the National Curriculum that have a direct bearing upon the relationship between science and humanities in the
secondary school curriculum, with a view to offering some tentative
suggestions as to how more collaborative approaches could be
developed across these two areas. This promises to be a daunting but
challenging task in that a number of difficulties are immediately
apparent.

Initially, the task is complicated by the degree of uncertainty
surrounding the final reports of the History and Geography Working Groups. At the time of writing, these reports have reached the
consultation stage but, in doing so, both have generated heated
debate and in the case of history, caused bitter professional divisions. Uncertainty was fuelled by Margaret Thatcher's pronounce-
ment in a *Sunday Telegraph* interview (12 April 1990) that she had
never intended the National Curriculum to extend beyond the core
subjects of English, mathematics and science and by widespread
press reports of rumours circulating within the Department of
Education and Science that, as a result of its contentiousness, the
Secretary of State is considering removing history from the National

Curriculum. Should this happen, it seems reasonable to assume that geography would be similarly treated. Meanwhile, in sharp contrast, science in the National Curriculum has reached a state of relative maturity and stability; its Attainment Targets and programmes of study have received Statutory Orders and these are now being implemented in schools.

A major conceptual difficulty is encountered in the attempt to establish an appropriate framework within which to examine the relationship between what might be seen as disparate, if not mutually incompatible, areas of the curriculum. This difficulty is exacerbated by the fact that whereas there appears to be an emerging consensus among science educators on what should constitute an appropriate science curriculum, in terms of both content and methodology, no such consensus exists in relation to humanities. On the contrary, the term 'humanities' itself is open to a range of interpretations, its meaning when applied to the school curriculum often differing markedly from the meaning implicit in its general academic usage. For example, philosophy and literature, by most definitions essential components of the humanities, are seldom included explicitly in the humanities curricula of secondary schools.

Difficulties are compounded by my personal concerns about the Education Reform Act in general and the imposition of a centrally prescribed National Curriculum in particular. These concerns are manifold and it is beyond the brief of this chapter to articulate them fully. However, as they have some bearing on later arguments, a brief résumé is appropriate. The imperatives of the Education Reform Act are primarily political and economic and are designed to subject all aspects of educational provision to a free-market ideology. The National Curriculum itself is conceptually muddled and philosophically naive. It fails to acknowledge that curricula are inherently political and value-laden or to recognize that the term 'curriculum' itself is problematic. Its emphasis on the tangible components of the curriculum, in terms of what it should cover and what the pupils should be taught, is indicative of a product conception of curriculum that belies the reality of curriculum as a 'contextualized social process' (Cornbleth, 1990). Stripped of rhetoric, its underlying premiss is that the curriculum consists of a hierarchy of subjects the content of which must be delivered to pupils by teachers. Consequently teachers are perceived as 'pedagogic civil servants' (Braham, 1988) whose professional expertise is confined to a mastery of the technical aspects of teaching and classroom management essential to the purveyance of state-sanctioned knowledge, and a command of the knowledge to be purveyed. This flies in the face of a tradition of educational research and curriculum innovation which has contributed to a more sophisticated understanding of education and the educational process.

It is not in the spirit of this book to dwell on the inadequacies of the National Curriculum but, rather, to search for positive ways forward within the framework it has established. Whatever the shortcomings, it has challenged many cherished assumptions and opened up the curriculum debate to a wider constituency. Even so, it is tempting to speculate that the National Curriculum will not survive for long in its present form but that it will eventually collapse under the weight of its inherent contradictions and practical shortcomings. With regular reports in the press of 'retreats' and 'climbdowns', there are indications that this is already beginning to happen. So it is imperative that thought be given not only to what is possible within present constraints but also to a consideration of what directions might be deemed appropriate, envisaging a future scenario of a more flexible structure.

As indicated earlier, there are major difficulties in delineating a humanities curriculum for there is no universally agreed definition of humanities. According to Eisner (1984), 'the variety of conceptions of the humanities are as diverse as the disciplines and fields of study that are said to constitute them', an observation that, ironically, in itself appears to embody certain contradictory assumptions. In schools in the twentieth century the demise of the classics, once the cornerstone of, if not synonymous with, humanities, and the corresponding emergence of the social sciences, adds further complications. Marx (1975) points out that 'no one has ever devised a clear set of distinctions for assigning some academic pursuits to the humanities and others to the social sciences', and Roberts (1984), similarly, draws attention to 'the endless confusion about the differences . . . between the humanities and the social sciences'. Jarrett (1973) observes that 'in England humanities often embraces, and is often slanted towards, the social sciences', a tendency which concerns White (1973) in that 'the sociologizing of the humanities curriculum undervalues the contemplative side of our nature'. Marx favours the adoption of a term like 'the study of man [*sic*]' or 'the human sciences' to describe the area of curriculum under discussion, since 'it may help to overcome the unfortunate cleavage between the humanities and the social sciences'.

In relation to the school curriculum, some progress through this minefield is possible by drawing a clear distinction between the conceptions of humanities implicit in the terms 'the humanities' and 'humanities'. The former implies a generic classification; an umbrella term embracing a number of disciplines which are considered discrete, if sometimes overlapping, entities. The latter, as its etymology suggests, used descriptively and in a singular sense, defines a broad area of enquiry which takes humanity or 'the human condition' as its central focus.

Historically, the generic conception of humanities as a collection of discrete subjects established itself firmly in the secondary school curriculum, with geography, history and religious studies being the dominant subjects. The desirability and legitimacy of this established orthodoxy has been challenged at various times, either by initiatives seeking more integrated approaches or by new subjects seeking a foothold in the curriculum. Early in the century, Mackinder (1913) advocated the teaching of geography and history as a combined subject on the grounds that subjects 'exist only in books and not in the real world'. The inter-war period saw the Association for Education in World Citizenship and its offshoot, the Council for Curriculum Reform, campaigning vigorously for the inclusion of additional subjects in the curriculum — notably political science and economics — to counteract the perceived threat of totalitarianism, and educational and social reconstruction in the immediate post-war era provided the context for the emergence of the social studies movement in the 1950s. Despite these challenges, geography and history, supported by powerful subject associations, have demonstrated remarkable resilience and considerable political acumen in maintaining their pre-eminence in the humanities curriculum. The position of religious education in the curriculum, of course, has been guaranteed by legislation since the 1944 Education Act.

From the mid-1960s onwards there have been continuing attempts by schools to reconstitute their humanities curricula. In this the tensions between the conflicting views of humanities outlined above have materialized in a plethora of 'integrated humanities' approaches, varying considerably in their radicalness and the degree to which they seek to 'integrate'. In some instances this has involved little more than a reorganization of the subject matter of the traditional core humanities subjects, perhaps accompanied by a token restructuring of the timetable. In others, there has been an attempt to broaden the humanities curriculum by the inclusion of additional subjects — or aspects of them — such as sociology, anthropology or economics, often chosen because of the insights they contribute to particular topics or human issues. Even though such approaches are potentially more integrative, subjects are still accorded status and distinctiveness in that they are deemed to have their own unique concepts, perspectives and methodologies. Consequently, the subject-based conception of humanities remains largely unchallenged.

More radical approaches have involved a rejection of the assumptions underpinning a subject-based conception of humanities and have violated with impunity the boundaries of traditional school subjects. Based primarily on a fundamental re-examination of the purpose of education and of the nature of knowledge, these approaches argue that the curriculum should be planned from a consideration of the kinds of experience offered to the pupils rather than from the knowledge content they are to engage with. Thus questions of pedagogy, rather than subject content, are seen as the central foci of curriculum planning. Such assumptions underpinned many of the nationally disseminated humanities projects of the 1970s, developed under the auspices of the Schools Council. The Keele Integrated Studies Project, for example, examined the possibilities of integration in the humanities area of the curriculum and sought ways of relating knowledge to the experiences, feelings and beliefs of the students. Similarly, the Humanities Curriculum Project, building on the practices of the 'innovatory secondary modern school' (Elliott, 1983) and based largely on the educational ideas of Lawrence Stenhouse, constructed a humanities curriculum around a number of controversial issues considered to be closely related to the lived experiences and practical concerns of the adolescent pupil. Moreover, this project made an explicit commitment to a set of pedagogical principles that encouraged the pupils to exercise their own judgement and express their own feelings about the significance of the topics and materials with which they engaged.

The Schools Council's humanities projects, together with other nationally disseminated projects such as Bruner's 'Man: A Course of Study' (Bruner, 1965) although not particularly 'successful' in terms of take-up, provided the impetus and expertise for the development of a number of innovatory school-based initiatives. The most successful of these furthei highlighted the artificiality and arbitrariness of the traditional subject-based conception of the humanities curriculum and the sterility of the learning experiences it often engenders. Unfortunately, the educational benefits of these courses have not always been appreciated, as invariably they are evaluated from a subject-based perspective. Nowhere is this more evident than in the inspection of integrated humanities courses by HMI. Furthermore, without 'any clear criteria for membership' (Black, 1975) and with 'no effective professional constituency' (Eisner, 1984), the development of humanities as a general field of study in its own right has met strong resistance from, and provided easy prey for, the powerful single-subject associations, for 'no fortified and protected interest readily surrenders any monopoly it may possess' (Dewey, 1966).

Schools committed to a more radical 'integrated' humanities curriculum often try to legitimize and defend their position by arguing that subjects are arbitrary socio-historical conventions rather than immutable logical necessities. Thus it becomes pertinent to ask what ideologies subjects embody and in whose interest and by what means they are maintained. This social-constructionist (Goodson, 1990) interpretation of the curriculum is readily acknowledged by many subject specialists. Johnston (1985), for example, points out that 'there is no "natural" discipline of geography . . . nor of any other social science' and Worsley (1985) comments that 'subject boundaries are created for administrative purposes and as such are artefacts'. The implications of this interpretation are far-reaching. It serves to highlight that the school curriculum, as a socio-historical construct, is inherently political and that the promotion of any one area or subject will mean campaigning against the interests of others — hence Goodson's (1983) contention that 'much of the curriculum debate can be interpreted in terms of conflicts between subjects over status resources and territory'. At the same time it provides legitimation for those endeavours that seek to deconstruct established curriculum patterns and create alternative configurations and alliances.

A central concern of this chapter is an examination of the changing balance both between and within science and humanities in the secondary school curriculum following the implementation of the National Curriculum in maintained schools in England and Wales as required by the 1988 Education Reform Act. The first section of the Act states that every pupil in maintained schools is entitled to a curriculum which is 'balanced and broadly based'. As a general principle, few would take issue with this statement. How this principle is interpreted and acted upon at the level of curriculum construction is another matter. When applied to the curriculum, the term 'breadth' is invariably used to delineate the range of experiences, however defined, to which the pupils are to be exposed and the term 'balance' to judge the appropriate weighting both within and between the various elements which comprise this range. The concepts of balance and breadth have been analysed extensively in educational literature and what has emerged from this analysis is a clear recognition of their complexity and contentiousness. Moreover, interpretations of the concepts vary markedly, contingent upon the epistemological position from which they are made (Kelly, 1986). As Rolls (1984) points out:

> there is no intellectually respectable argument for a balanced curriculum which is not predicated on views of the nature of Man, of knowledge, of society or of some amalgam of these.

It is evident that little understanding of the nuances of this debate penetrated the consciousness of those responsible for formulating the overall framework of the National Curriculum for, in doing so, they never made explicit the criteria by which their conception of a balanced and broadly based curriculum was to be rendered meaningful. In the absence of any contrary explanation, and in light of the curriculum they subsequently endorsed, it seems reasonable to infer that, in their view, a balanced and broadly based curriculum is to be judged by reference to the range of traditional academic subjects included. The inadequacies of this are now abundantly clear as the National Curriculum Council endeavours to make good what are seen as serious omissions by bolting on an elaborate, but conceptually flawed, impractical and ever-changing, structure of 'cross-curricular elements' in terms of 'dimensions, skills and themes' (NCC, 1989). Having created this unwieldly edifice, the government has no option but to defend it, even though its deficiencies are becoming increasingly apparent.

Little would be gained at this stage by embarking on further analysis of the concepts of balance and breadth or by attempting to elucidate an alternative framework within which a broad and balanced curriculum might be realized. Such frameworks already exist; examples are the eight areas of experience proposed by HMI (DES, 1976), recently reiterated in a slightly revised form by the National Union of Teachers (NUT, 1990), Eisner's (1982) 'modes of representation' and Lawton's (1989) 'cultural invarients'. Although not without their own conceptual problems, potentially they offer more coherent frameworks for curriculum planning than the ten core and foundation subjects of the National Curriculum in that they imply that it is the experiences of the learners and the processes of learning, rather than subject content, that lie at the heart of human development.

In light of the foregoing arguments, it seems reasonable to conclude that trying to delineate a broad and balanced curriculum in any definitive sense is as futile as searching for the Holy Grail. Such utopian approaches to curriculum construction inevitably raise more questions than they resolve. A more pragmatic, and potentially more fruitful, approach concentrates on highlighting and systematically eliminating instances of imbalance in the curriculum as they become evident. Applying this logic to the National Curriculum, a number of imbalances are immediately discernible, both in its overall structure and within its component parts. These imbalances are manifested at various levels and in a number of ways and they have far-reaching implications for the humanities curriculum and its relation to the curriculum as a whole. The degree to which they are exacerbated or alleviated will depend to a large extent on how the National Curriculum is interpreted and implemented at the school level. The remainder of this chapter is devoted to an analysis of these issues.

In its overall structure the National Curriculum is imbalanced in that it assumes hierarchies in its component parts. Within this hierarchy, humanities and arts are accorded low priority and status in relation to the core subjects of English, maths and science. More specifically, a humanities curriculum formulated almost exclusively in terms of history and geography lacks balance and breadth because it denies pupils access to a range of important political, social, moral and spiritual experiences which fall outside the concerns of these subjects.

At the level of individual subjects, imbalances are inherent in the predominantly ethnocentric and patriarchal interpretations of geography and history by the respective National Curriculum working groups and in the requirement of the Reform Act that religious education syllabuses 'shall reflect the fact that the religious traditions in Great Britain are in the main Christian' (HMSO, 1988). In the case of geography, imbalance is further accentuated by the commitment of the Working Group to reaffirm 'the place and status of the physical and scientific elements of geographical studies' while, at the same time, playing down geography's links with humanities by asserting that the skills of the subject are more closely related to mathematic and scientific skills than they are to the skills of history.

In relation to the concerns of this chapter, questions on the nature of geography and its place in the National Curriculum are of particular significance. The general thrust of the report of the Geography Working Group reflects and reinforces a general aspiration of geographers, often in a misguided search for academic respectability, to align their subject substantially, if not wholly, with science rather than humanities. This aspiration found its ultimate expression in the so-called quantitative revolution of the 1950s and 1960s. Characterized by increased attention to theoretical considerations and the use of mathematics in quantification and model-building (Beaver, 1982), it sought to recast geography as a law-seeking discipline, utilizing the principles and methods of positive science.

Although there has been a reaction against and a drift away from positivism within the social sciences generally, its legacy persists powerfully in secondary school geography curricula. Its basic precepts pervade many textbooks and examination syllabuses (Gilbert, 1984) and are unavoidably built into much of the geography computer software. The preoccupation of HMI in *Geography 5–16* (DES, 1986) with 'the spatial', in terms of 'patterns', 'processes', 'generalizations', 'models', 'interactions', 'linkages', 'locations' and 'relationships', together with reified notions such as 'modes', 'location quotient', 'least cost locations', 'comparative advantage', 'social costs' and 'best locations', provides further indication of its pervasive influence. Such a perspective is antithetical to humanities in that, predicated upon the predictability of human behaviour, it denies the subjectivity of human experience and the creative power of human intentionality and free will. In the context of the school curriculum, the excessive bias towards a positivistic view of geography provides little scope, let alone encouragement, for the development of those critical and phenomenological/existentialist perspectives associated with radical and humanistic geographies respectively; perspectives, moreover, which have far greater potential for incorporating the learners' own experiences, perceptions and values into the educational process.

Geography often asserts its distinctiveness as an academic subject on the grounds that it is an 'integrative' or 'synthesizing' subject which 'creates a bridge between the sciences and humanities' (DES, 1990a). The Geographical Association (1989) claims that 'any meaningful study of human activity must, therefore, be founded on a soundly based understanding of the physical environment'. For Orme (1985), 'geography without a physical base is sociology'. These views, although widespread, are not shared by all geographers. Norton (1989), for example, claims that they are based on assertion, not logic, and that geography has failed to demonstrate a physical–human unity. Likewise, Johnston (1983) finds 'the links between physical and human geography tenuous', as they are 'separate fields each overlapping more with other fields than with each other', and Worsley (1985) contends that 'experience has led [him] to the conviction that physical geography has its most important affinities with the earth sciences'. The 'bridging' claims of geography, even if justified on epistemological grounds, may, of course, bear little relation to actual classroom practice. Indeed, pupils' experience of the subject often consists of little more than passive exposure to a range of unrelated topics held together by convention and habit rather than by any clearly articulated epistemological or educational rationale.

So far in this chapter attention has focused primarily on issues relating to the humanities curriculum. During the 1980s there have been a number of significant developments in science education which have profound implications for its relationship with other areas of the curriculum in general and humanities in particular. As claimed earlier, there is an emerging consensus on what should constitute an appropriate science curriculum, a consensus, moreover, unmatched in any other curriculum area (Carpenter, 1987). The Royal Society report (1982) foreshadowed the DES policy statement (1985) in recommending balanced science for all, a recommendation that subsequently became a consistent part of the Secondary Science Curriculum Review's proposals for the science curriculum. The translation of this policy into practice has led to a number of different curricular arrangements which are generally described as coordinated, combined, modular and integrated. Coordinated and combined courses retain clearly identifiable strands of biology, chemistry and physics but are organized in such a way that links between the subjects are highlighted and reinforced. Modular courses arrange the content, whether single subject or interdisciplinary, into discrete units. Integrated courses blur traditional boundaries between subjects by structuring the learning experiences around key ideas or themes which emphasize the unity of science (DES, 1990a). It is interesting to note that these curricular arrangements have much in common with the various approaches that have been adopted for organizing the humanities curriculum, as described by Williams (1984). And it is ironic that while the science curriculum moves confidently into the 1990s on a 'balanced science for all' ticket the humanities curriculum fragments as the constitutive subjects compete aggressively with each other for the few crumbs that are left after the more prestigious core subjects — including science — have secured their share of time and resources.

In terms of content, there have been attempts to broaden the science curriculum beyond the traditional biology–chemistry–physics tritarian base. For example, the Secondary Science Curriculum Review (1987) recommended that, in addition to biology, chemistry and physics, science studies should include elements of astronomy, computer science, earth science, electronics and technology. More significantly, in compiling a contents list a range of topics were included which could be seen as violating established curriculum boundaries — for example, biosphere, communication, health, lithosphere and physical landscape, population growth, relationships and weather.

The content of the science curriculum has been further influenced by a commitment to make it more accessible to the learners and more relevant to their needs, interests and lived experiences. There are parallels here with the aspirations of the more radical integrated humanities initiatives described earlier. Consequently, there has been a move away from a view of science education as primarily the acquisition of a body of verified knowledge — and an understanding of the procedures by which it is verified — to one which emphasizes an engagement with the processes of science and the study of science as a cultural activity. Thus, in the 1980s, science policy statements and curricular initiatives have placed greater emphasis on the study of the philosophy and history of science, on its political, moral and economic implications and on its technological applications and the social, cultural and environmental consequences of these.

In schools with a commitment to promoting greater social justice and equality, the science curriculum has been profoundly influenced by the adoption of anti-racist and anti-sexist teaching strategies. In relation to science education, such strategies begin from the premiss that as science is located and practised within the wider context of Western capitalism it is inherently exploitative, a view forcefully expressed by Seamon (1984):

> The manipulative, explanatory, predictive style of positivist science clearly parallels the masculine, centralized, materialist power structures which not only subjugate minorities and even national populations but also manipulate and exploit the natural environment bringing on ecological damage and collapse.

So there is a need for the science curriculum to explicate and subject to critical examination the political, economic and social interests and priorities that inform science itself. The pursuit of this goal has led to more holistic and person-centred forms of enquiry which challenge the reductionist assumptions of positivist science.

In terms of pedagogy, science education has been transformed in many schools by the adoption of a constructivist view of learning. This view sees the learner as an active agent in the construction of his/her own knowledge and so recognizes the need to utilize the conceptual framework the learner already possesses as the starting point in the development of his/her scientific understanding. This has resulted in the adoption of a pedagogy which places greater emphasis on interactive forms of learning. Within this framework, pupils, working collaboratively, are encouraged to formulate and test hypotheses and draw conclusions, discuss ideas and exchange points of view, make judgements and explore values.

It would be misleading to suggest that these developments are widely practised or that they have received universal acclaim. On the contrary, within science education they have been largely marginalized and when viewed from a humanities perspective they are perceived by some as a potential threat. The National Curriculum Geography Working Group in its interim report (DES, 1989a) claimed that the science Attainment Targets AT 5 (Human Influences on the Earth) and AT 9 (Earth and Atmosphere) 'impinge on geography' and in the final report (DES, 1990b) it requested 'the removal of any essentially geographical material from the science attainment targets and programmes of study'. Likewise, Storm alludes to the 'intellectually megalomaniacal science proposals' (1989a) and the 'gargantuan claim of science to encompass just about everything' (1989b) and, in doing so, echoes similar concerns expressed at the beginning of the century when A. F. Pollard accused scientists of wanting 'not a place in the sun but control of the sunshine' (cited in Gordon, 1984). Furthermore, he doubted whether science teachers 'have the expertise and experience to develop effective studies of people/environment interactions', conveniently ignoring, of course, the inability of many geography teachers to deal with scientific concepts other than at a superficial level.

Such concerns are ill-founded in that they reflect the narrow, vested interests of subject specialists, rather than the wider educational interests of the pupils they teach. Moreover, they often rest upon a distorted image of scientific enquiry — one implicit in many science curricula — as the disinterested pursuit of value-free objective knowledge in accordance with the canons and internal logic of 'the scientific method' and detached from, and untainted by, the socio-political context in which it is embedded. By reinforcing the view that humanities has a monopoly on the socio-political, moral and spiritual dimensions of human experience, they serve to perpetuate the 'two cultures' mentality so eloquently and forcefully articulated by C. P. Snow (1969). There is a need for a wider recognition that many science educators readily endorse curricula which embody an acknowledgement of human agency in the scientific enterprise and that they consider an engagement with questions of value to be an integral part of science education. The developments described here constitute important and legitimate developments in science education which should be actively encouraged — not selfishly opposed by vested subject interests — in that they have the potential to broaden the concept of the humanities curriculum and go some way to redressing the imbalances that are inherent in the overall structure of the National Curriculum. As Eisner (1984) argues, 'even those areas of the curriculum that appear most remote from the humanities could be studied for their humanistic potential'. Kliebard (1984) agrees. For him the promotion of humanistic study lies not in a qualitative shift in the balance of humanities and science in the curriculum but 'primarily in reconstituting all the studies that comprise the curriculum so that their origins in human purposes and human activity are restored and made the focal point of study'.

The most significant feature to emerge from this analysis is the striking commonality of purpose between the innovatory humanities projects and the recent developments in science education. This could be summarized as:

a commitment to interactive forms of learning which value and start from the experiences and knowledge of the pupils;

a commitment to helping pupils gain understanding of the processes by which knowledge is constructed and insight into the social and political context in which this takes place;

a focus on issues of social significance that are relevant to the needs, interests and concerns of the pupils.

In addition to promoting a more humanistic conception of science, in terms of both content and pedagogy, the Secondary Science Curriculum Review (1983) openly invited and actively encouraged closer working relationships with other areas of the curriculum. The degree to which this has been reciprocated is a moot point! Contrary to expectations, the National Curriculum has opened up numerous possibilities for developing the kinds of cross-curricular initiative they envisaged, for as the various working groups have defined their subjects areas of common interest have been accentuated. Provided territorial disputes can be resolved, there is considerable potential for collaborative ventures between geography and science, particularly in relation to earth science and environmental education. At present, physical geography is taught largely through the blackboard, textbooks, visual aids, maps and the occasional fieldwork and, as such, would be greatly enhanced by laboratory-based experimental work.

The much maligned American social studies project (Bruner, 1965) 'Man: A Course of Study' (MACOS) — although now a rare and endangered species in British schools — when successfully practised provided an exemplar of effective integration of the biological and human sciences. A major feature of this project was an exploration of the dynamic relation between culture and technology within the wider context of contrasting belief systems. Moreover, built around the substantive question 'what makes humans human?', the project afforded opportunities for the study of the self and of the process of becoming a person in ways which drew upon both scientific and humanistic understanding. This reference to MACOS should not be interpreted as a call for a return to some mythologized past, but as an attempt to illustrate the kinds of collaborative activity that could be developed in the future within — at least for the time being — the parameters set by the National Curriculum.

The National Curriculum History Working Group in its final report identifies 'economic, technological and scientific' as one of the four dimensions of historical knowledge. This provides a suitable framework for studying the history of science in ways that highlight its technological applications, socio-cultural consequences and moral dilemmas. Some of the proposed History Study Units, such as HSU 11 (The Development of Writing and Printing) and HSU 12 (Land Transport through History), have a distinct science/technological focus although, unfortunately from a secondary perspective, most of these are designated to key stage 2. Other proposed units, such as HSU 25 (Islamic Civilization up to the Early Sixteenth Century), offer an ideal context for developing materials which challenge the white, ethnocentric image of science. Clearly there is considerable overlap between the history proposals and AT 17 (the nature of science) of the Science National Curriculum.

Thus it can be seen that the National Curriculum, although formulated in terms of subjects, provides opportunities for active collaboration and new syntheses across science and humanities in the secondary school curriculum. Peters (1975) claimed that 'education should, above all things, sensitize us to the predicaments in which we are placed as human beings'. More recently, Maxwell (1984) called for a new kind of intellectual enquiry devoted to the enhancement of wisdom in respect of the personal and social problems encountered in our lives as we strive to realize that which is desirable and of value. As we move towards the twenty-first century, it becomes increasingly obvious that the predicament and problems we face in pursuit of 'the good' do not fit neatly into traditional subject categories. It is imperative that we engage in a fundamental reappraisal of the epistemological and pedagogical assumptions underpinning the school curriculum. The realization of this in practice will depend largely upon the vision and commitment of teachers and upon their willingness to engage open-mindedly with colleagues on new, collaborative ventures.

we hope to have passed beyond the stage of either scientists or humanists thinking that they alone represent the truth and the light.

(Jarrett, 1983)

BIBLIOGRAPHY

Beaver, S. H. (1982) Geography in the British Association for the Advancement of Science. *The Geographical Journal*, **148**(2), 173–181.

Black, M. (1975) Some tasks for the humanities, in Niblett, W. R. (ed.) *The Sciences, the Humanities and the Technological Threat*. London: University of London Press.

Braham, M. (1988) The ecology of education, in Briceno, S. and Pitt, D. C. (eds) *New Ideas in Environmental Education*. London: Croom Helm.

Bruner, J. S. (1965) Man: A Course of Study. *Education Services Inc.* Quarterly Report (Spring–Summer), pp. 3–13.

Carpenter, I. (1987) Balanced science for all: where are we now? *The Times Educational Supplement*, 3 April, p. 12.

Cornbleth, C. (1990) *Curriculum in Context*. London: Falmer Press.

DES [Department of Education and Science] (1976) *Curriculum 11–16*. London: HMSO.

DES [Department of Education and Science] (1985) *Science 5–16: A Statement of Policy*. London: HMSO.

DES [Department of Education and Science] (1986) *Geography 5–16*. London: HMSO.

DES [Department of Education and Science] (1989a) *National Curriculum Geography Working Group: Interim Report*. London: HMSO.

DES [Department of Education and Science] (1989b) *Science in the National Curriculum*. London: HMSO.

DES [Department of Education and Science] (1990a) *A Survey of Balanced Science Courses in Some Secondary Schools*. London: HMSO.

DES [Department of Education and Science] (1990b) *Geography for Ages 5 to 16*. London: HMSO.

DES [Department of Education and Science] (1990c) *History from Ages 5 to 16*. London: HMSO.

Dewey, J. (1966) *Democracy and Education*. New York: The Free Press; first published 1916.

Eisner, E. (1982) *Cognition and Curriculum*. London and New York: Longman.

Eisner, E. (1984) Can the humanities be taught in American public schools? in Lander, B. (ed.) *The Humanities in Precollegiate Education*. Chicago: University of Chicago Press.

Elliott, J. (1983) A curriculum for the study of human affairs: the contribution of Lawrence Stenhouse. *Journal of Curriculum Studies*, **15**(2), 105–23.

Geographical Association (1989) *Physical Geography in the School Curriculum*. Sheffield: Geographical Association.

Gilbert, R. (1984) *The Impotent Image*. London: Falmer Press.

Goodson, I. (1983) *School Subjects and Curriculum Change*. London: Croom Helm.

Goodson, I. (1990) Studying curriculum: towards a social constructionist perspective. *Journal of Curriculum Studies*, **22**(4), 299–312.

Gordon, P. (1984) *Purpose and Planning in the Humanities Curriculum*. London: Institute of Education.

HMSO (1988) *The Education Reform Act*. London: HMSO.

Jarrett, J. R. (1973) *The Humanities and Humanistic Education*. Reading, Mass.: Addison-Wesley.

Johnston, R. J. (1983) *Geography and Geographers*. London: Edward Arnold.

Johnston, R. J. (1984) *On Human Geography*. Oxford: Basil Blackwell.

Johnston, R. J. (ed.) (1985) *The Future of Geography*. London: Methuen.

Kelly, A. V. (1986) *Knowledge and Curriculum Planning*. London: Harper & Row.

Kliebard, H. M. (1984) The decline of humanistic study in the American school curriculum. In Lander, B. (ed.) *The Humanities in Precollegiate Education*. Chicago: University of Chicago Press.

Lawton, D. (1989) *Education, Culture and the National Curriculum*. London: Hodder & Stoughton.

Mackinder, H. (1913) Teaching geography and history as a combined subject. *The Geography Teacher*, **7**, 4–9.

Marx, L. (1975) Technology and the study of man. In Niblett, W. R. (ed.) *The Sciences, the Humanities and the Technological Threat*. London: University of London Press.

Maxwell, N. (1984) *From Knowledge to Wisdom*. Oxford: Basil Blackwell.

National Union of Teachers (1990) *A Strategy for the Curriculum*. London: NUT.

NCC [National Curriculum Council] (1989) *The National Curriculum and Whole Curriculum Planning. Primary Guidance*. York: National Curriculum Council. (Circular no. 6).

Norton, W. (1989) Human geography and the geographical imagination. *Journal of Geography*, **88**(5), 186–92.

Orme, A. (1985) Understanding and predicting the physical world. In Johnston, R. J. (ed.) *The Future of Geography*. London: Methuen.

Peters, R. S. (1975) Subjectivity and standards. In Niblett, W. R. (ed.) *The Sciences, the Humanities and the Technological Threat*. London: University of London Press.

Roberts, F. (1984) Precollegiate humanities: leadership curriculum issues. In Lander, B. (ed.) *The Humanities in Precollegiate Education*. Chicago: University of Chicago Press.

Rolls, I. (1984) The future of science education: an alternative perspective. *School Science Review*, **65**(232), 429–39.

Royal Society (1982) *Report on Science Education 11–16 in England and Wales*. London: The Royal Society.

Seamon, D. (1984) The question of reliable knowledge: the irony and tragedy of positivist research. *The Professional Geographer*, **36**, 216–18.

Snow, C. P. (1969) *The Two Cultures: A Second Look*. Cambridge: Cambridge University Press.

SSCR [Secondary *Science* Curriculum Review] (1983) *Science Education 11–16: Proposals for Action and Consultation*. London: Heinemann/ Association for Science Education for the Schools Curriculum Development Committee.

SSCR [Secondary *Science* Curriculum Review] (1987) *Better Science: Choosing Content*. London: Heinemann/Association for Science Education for the Schools Curriculum Development Committee.

Storm, M. (1989a) World view. *Teacher*, 1 May.

Storm, M. (1989b) Geography and the National Curriculum. *Teaching Geography*, **14**(3).

White, J. (1973) *Towards a Compulsory Curriculum*. London: Routledge & Kegan Paul.

Williams, M. (1984) *Designing and Teaching Integrated Courses*. Sheffield: Geographical Association.

Worsley, P. (1985) Physical geography and the natural environmental sciences. In Johnston, R. J. (ed.) *The Future of Geography*. London: Methuen.

Chapter 6

Science and the Creative Arts

Della West

A hush descends on the audience as the curtain parts to reveal three cylinders isolated by spotlights and a huddle of tangled shapes covered by black plastic. Voices can be heard beneath the plastic which begins to move, eventually being thrown roughly aside to reveal human-sized representations of a banana skin, a plastic washing-up-liquid bottle and a newspaper. From within the cylinders emerge a bottle, an aluminium can and folds of computer paper, all giant sized and very vocal. The drama has begun and so has the science for performer and audience alike! Theatre in Education (TIE) has long been seen as a most effective means of introducing a topic or examining an issue, with adults as performers and pupils as spectators, but what if the pupils were the performers of a drama devised by them, researched by them and presented to other students or an adult audience?

Drama, of course, is not included as a separate subject under the National Curriculum and many may consider that its inclusion here is yet another attempt to justify its existence. This is not necessary, for where good practice exists in drama in schools it is recognized as having great value in helping pupils to greater social and personal awareness and understanding, in addition to knowledge of a powerful art form. The emphasis should be on the value to the pupils' learning experience and not to departmental politics. Drama can provide the medium for a 'meaningful learning experience' if the process is well planned and effectively handled. There is, then, surely even greater value if the work done in drama not only helps pupils' personal, social and creative development but contributes to their knowledge and understanding of another curriculum area. Few would question using a historical stimulus for drama work so why not a scientific one too?

Cynics might feel that this approach reduces drama to the level of a service subject but that is not the basis upon which this chapter is presented. Drama looks to many areas of the curriculum for interesting material and even the NCC has recognized the value of drama in the teaching of science by including it specifically in the range of teaching strategies, applicable specifically to OAT 17:

- when pupils act out incidents the experience can help them remember and learn more effectively. It can also be useful for simulating the different social conditions in which the scientific ideas arose, and motivate those pupils whose special talents are not usually employed in science lessons. Drama will probably not involve acting a set piece, or learning set lines; it is better when it includes a large measure of improvisation.
- the replication of historical experiments accompanied by a group argument about how the results should be interpreted, is another useful form of drama.
- simulation or role play is a third kind of drama which is particularly useful for examining the scientific, economic, social and cultural aspects of technological decision making. Carrying out a role play debate about what kind of power station to build (AT 13 L8) will introduce economic and social issues. If the location is in a Third World country an interesting multicultural element will also be involved.

(NCC, 1989)

I feel there is a fourth area which can be added here: pupils find it helpful to create the behaviour of molecules when looking at physical reactions — this can often come under the title of movement or even dance, though it is perhaps an extreme form of role play to behave like a hydrogen atom!

There are, then, several ways in which drama can be used:

1. Drama techniques can be used by the science specialist within the science lesson.
2. Scientific material, which pupils have worked on in science, is used by the drama teacher for exploration in the drama lesson.

But these two keep the science and drama apart. Many pupils might feel better motivated if:

3. Drama is used as a stimulus for the learning.

4.   Then a joint framework is established in which the work takes place as a parallel development in science and drama.

In the primary years approaches 3 and 4 are more easily attainable, but as the compartmentalized timetable in secondary schools is felt to work against this, approach 1 and/or 2 may be best.

All require that exploration of the possibilities and the planning take place within a cross-curricular staff grouping, for in each case there is likely to be an 'information gap' sustained over past years by the arts v. sciences divide in education itself. The problem has been set in context by the NCC Arts in Schools project:

49 — A distinction is often taken for granted between the arts & sciences. Sometimes, these are seen as opposites, even opponents. The sciences and technology tend to be associated with intellectual and practical achievements respectively, the arts with feelings, emotions and recreation. This apparent dichotomy between the arts and sciences is comparatively recent. Its roots lie in the intellectual revolutions in philosophy, mathematics and sciences which erupted in Europe during the seventeenth century and in the technological revolution that followed during the eighteenth and nineteenth centuries. Progressively during this period science came to be associated with 'objective fact', and, through its impact on technology, with confronting the practicalities of the 'real' world. The arts by contrast became associated with less worldly concerns: with beauty, values, feelings and 'culture'.

50 — New inputs into the nature of human perception and intelligence, and developments in the philosophy of science and of the arts have begun to dissolve these dichotomies and to reestablish the relationships between artistic, scientific and other modes of understanding. The sciences have many characteristics that have come to be almost exclusively associated with the arts and vice versa.

One has only to take a brief look at the history of science to recognize that often a scientist's creativity has led to advancement. The converse is also true, for the arts require tight discipline in the acquisition and application of skills. Therefore if true cross-curricular work is to be attained, the arts and sciences will need to recognize these common strands and open the dialogue — a process which can only be of value to all concerned.

Drama does not have a specific National Curriculum (NC) document of its own but is bound up in the Speaking and Listening and Reading sections of the English orders (which are dealt with in a separate chapter). A useful publication aimed specifically at drama teaching in schools is *Curriculum Matters 17: Drama from 5 to 16* (HMI, 1989), for it is here that the teacher is urged to attend to 'the potentially dynamic relationship of drama to other foundation subjects of the National Curriculum'. It might be useful here to consider that relationship with science.

The first aim of learning through drama is identified: 'through their work pupils should understand the educational, cultural and social purposes of drama'. This aim is echoed in the introductory paragraph to the National Curriculum Science Attainment Target 17, 'The Nature of Science':

> Pupils should develop their knowledge and understanding of the ways in which scientific ideas change through time and how the nature of these ideas and the uses to which they are put are affected by the contexts in which they are developed; in doing so they should begin to recognise that while science is an important way of thinking about experience it is not the only way.

This aim is also strongly underlined by the section 'The Contribution of Science to the Curriculum' (4.3) (NCC, 1989, p. 123):

> Appreciating the contribution science makes to society will encourage pupils to develop a sense of their responsibilities as members of society and of the contributions they can make to it. A study of some of the moral and ethical issues raised by developing technology can bring added awareness of the wider issues and difficulties involved in the application of science in the developing and the developed world.

Dramatic aims are focused on the suggestion that pupils should:

- '• use a range of dramatic forms to express ideas and feelings.
- • appreciate drama in performance both as participants and spectators.'

These are reflected in NC Science in 'Learning Science', 6.5 'Pupils' scientific ideas do not develop only through first-hand experiences. Communication with others plays an important part in the learning process.' This 'communication' can take many forms and it is at this point that the science and the drama can effectively interact.

The general educational purposes outlined in *Drama from 5 to 16* echo many of the points made to illustrate the fact that learning in science contributes to personal development: the dramatic 'explore' becomes a scientific request to 'combine interest with curiosity'; to 'learn to respect and, where necessary, depend upon others' compares with 'respect for living organisms' and 'a responsible attitude to health and safety'; to 'develop awareness and enjoyment of the ways groups work' becomes 'co-operation with others'; and finally, to 'evaluate their achievements as individuals and through the groups in which they work', as well as to 'appreciate the values of their own, and other, communities' translates into developing 'understanding and clarifying one's own thinking'.

The echoes continue in the Drama learning objectives outlined at ages 7, 11 and 16 (HMI, 1989).

At age 7, it is hoped that pupils will:

identify with characters and actions through role playing, for instance a dramatised story and as spectators of a live performance
learn to work together to solve human and practical problems
explore the differences between right and wrong in simple moral dilemmas posed through drama

At age 11 pupils should

invent and develop convincing roles in specific situations
create and take part in improvised scenes in order to explore particular issues which could, for instance have a practical, social or moral dimension
select and use first hand material which is relevant and dramatically significant

At age 16 they should

integrate sound and silence, movement and stillness, light and darkness to make effective use of spaces where dramatic action takes place
create improvised or written drama for others

Compare these points with the criteria for selecting particular learning experiences for pupils. Teachers of science are asked that their work might give pupils the opportunity to:

develop attitudes appropriate to working scientifically
develop basic scientific concepts
reach a satisfactory outcome
apply scientific ideas to real-life problems
work co-operatively and communicate scientific ideas to others
develop an understanding of the relationship of scientific ideas to spiritual, ethical and moral dilemmas
discuss the ways in which scientists work

Indeed, in the non-statutory guidance (NCC, 1989) there seems a demand that pupils should have the opportunity to develop increasing independence and the chance to take responsibility for their own learning where they are enabled to:

- divide into groups
- agree upon individual responsibilities
- decide upon objectives
- carry out the task
- collect data
- analyse and interpret
- evaluate and draw conclusions
- communicate to others

This could be a plan for a drama lesson, too!

Once common ground underlying the learning of drama and science has been established, it is vital that one appreciates the elements of learning that are felt to be acquired and developed in the aims and objectives for drama and how these relate to learning opportunities for science. The five specific areas outlined in *Drama from 5 to 16* (HMI, 1989) are

concepts
knowledge and understanding
imagination
skills
attitudes

These five elements of learning in drama can be brought to bear in a scientific context.

The concepts of drama provide the teacher with the tools to allow the pupil to shape the drama into a communicable form. In pretending to be someone they are not, they are creating a fiction, an imagined world which they control and within which symbols may be used to create such ideas as status and power. For example, a stethoscope might be useful to identify a doctor, a helmet a policeman. Character and role can allow pupils to explore, within the fiction, the experience of an individual, his thoughts and feelings. He can then step out of that character and examine the experience for himself. For example, if enacting the role of a farmer who uses pesticides and insecticides on his crops, having to justify his actions in an interview on an 'open-forum' discussion programme might help a pupil reflect on his responses as acceptable or unacceptable, justified or not, morally and socially. The situation or setting in which the drama takes place can help pupils create the social and historic climate against which and within which to work. What would a seventeenth-century laboratory have contained? This question could be used to stimulate the construction, with the whole group contributing ideas, of an imagined setting for role play to work in. This process would help to build the context in which the drama is to be placed, thus stimulating a greater depth of understanding. The rules and conventions of the drama help create its meanings, control them and communicate them. They are used to shape the delivery of material to an audience. For example, a pantomime of Jack and the Beanstalk might be an ideal means of exploring the idea of the requirement for growth in plants for older pupils and then communicating the information in the pantomime mode to a group of younger pupils (Bishop David Brown School, Woking, Surrey SATRO Science and Drama Competition, Epsom Playhouse, 1990).

In extending the knowledge and understanding of pupils, drama enables the bringing to life of knowledge and experience that might otherwise be inert. In using drama in science, specific types of knowledge and understanding can be identified.

1. Pupils' own experience of the world around them provides the most powerful starting point which can be extended through the use of imagination. All pupils can observe the changes which take place from ice to liquid to water vapour; imagination can help them speculate, using their bodies as molecules, on the behaviour and relationship of hydrogen and oxygen in each of the states. Some suitable sound accompaniment, vocal or instrumental, recorded or live, could underline and complete an experience that is unlikely to be forgotten — for it has not been learned as a dry fact but has been 'experienced'.

2. Historical source material might be required but the facts would be used to equip the pupils with an understanding of the attitudes, values, feelings, personalities and problems of the time. To understand the situation in which Galileo found himself, pupils would need to understand the beliefs of the Church about the universe at that time and the observations made by Galileo. Pupils would need to develop an understanding of his life and the lives of the people around him for the drama to work.

The value of imagination in allowing pupils to draw factual information into role play or the building of settings is unquestionable, foi it allows the pupil to leap into a role and a world of which she is a part and then, when it is done, she can return to the real world, the real person.

The skills of drama centre upon use of language appropriate to the situation, the development of the voice, the ability to move effectively and finally the use of technical resources to add impact to the drama. These can all be brought into play in even the humblest of drama activities.

Finally, attitudes. Here it is appropriate to give the list of attitudes and personal qualities felt to be 'important at all stages of science education':

curiosity
respect for evidence
willingness to tolerate uncertainty
critical reflection
perseverance
creativity and inventiveness
open-mindedness
sensitivity to the living and the non-living environment
co-operation with others

This list could equally be labelled 'important for drama education', and accepted as such.

At this point a distinction needs to be made between drama that takes place within the classroom, helping the pupils to assimilate information or concepts, and that allows manipulation of them for their own learning to take place, and drama that is developed for an audience, which might have arisen out of the first level of drama but carries a further purpose of communication with others.

Also one must not ignore the valuable contribution to pupils' understanding of science which can be made by an outside group — Theatre in Education projects such as The Molecule Club, or school-based drama-centred groups in need of an audience, for example SEG Creative Arts (Surrey modular) GCSE Drama in Education module. The latter example provides an ideal vehicle for cross-phase work, for example pupils at key stage 4 working on a presentation for pupils at key stages 1/2 on recycled materials. (The opening example of this chapter is taken from a piece developed by Year 10 pupils as part of their Drama in Education module for GCSE work.)

Having examined very carefully the areas of commonality between science and drama documentation, it is now necessary to look at the means by which the theory might be translated into practice. First, discussion can be entered into at different levels:

between individual members of one school's staff
between departments
cross-phase, within the feeder school's organization
cross-institution in consortium groups

The debate could be in any of these areas as a starting point, but it is hoped that all of them would eventually be included, in the interests of disseminating good practice. A curriculum audit, vital to establish the prevailing position in all curriculum areas, is the most desirable whole-school action. The responses to this can then be shared so that discussions and positive reactions can be made at the planning and formative stage in the process of restructuring schemes of work. But individual staff may choose to work as a pair in the first instance and, once confidence has been gained on both sides, moves could be made to encourage others to try out what is, for the science teacher, essentially a change in teaching and learning style.

A plea can be made here that the NCC documents are not only provided for their particular subject staff but for all staff, with the programmes of study seen as 'required reading' for all — those areas of experience which are not reported on by the NCC are assumed to be included here also. Thus staff as a whole can begin to identify areas of common ground across the curriculum.

It is important that teachers continue to provide meaningful learning experiences which satisfy the programmes of study and not teach to the Attainment Targets. The approach needs to be one of familiarizing a whole-school staff with the areas of study tackled in science from which all staff may be invited to respond to any section which might be seen as common ground or invite a positive response. Such a 'brainstorming' session can be so dynamically stimulating that the curriculum barriers tumble and staff may then explore common ground and share skills.

Such a whole-school approach is desirable, but may be considered unattainable. How might a department or an individual teacher proceed?

First there needs to be a recognition that drama can contribute something to the teaching of science. Next, the appropriate department or member of staff needs to be approached. So many drama teachers work in isolation in schools—particularly at secondary level—that most would welcome interest from other subject areas, not merely along the lines of 'I need your expertise' or 'I would like to use drama in my lessons', but rather 'I think you and I could share materials and learning strategies for our mutual benefit'.

In order to illustrate the possibilities of the drama–science link, it seems appropriate to choose an example worked in detail to demonstrate how one might proceed in practice, but it must be remembered that this was written for a particular pupil group in a particular school and would need to be considered carefully for another school's circumstance and tailored to the needs of its pupils.

EXAMPLE: THE HABER PROCESS

Fritz Haber won the Nobel prize for his work on fertilizers in 1918. He was a Jew, living, studying and working in Germany before Hitler's rise to power. From the process for the production of fertilizers, the work was taken on by another scientist to produce explosives required for the First World War. This story provides the ideal model of a scientific process developed for the progress of the world being used unscrupulously by powerful men for the world's destruction: the moral dilemma is a very strong one, the background very emotive, set as it is in such a rapidly changing world as Europe in the early twentieth century. The opportunities for learning in science exist at many levels within the attainment targets.

The work would be aimed at key stage 4.

An analysis of the detailed sections of the programmes of study covered by the work is included here. This demonstrates how dealing with work in this way covers a range of Attainment Targets within the development of the scientific and dramatic aspects of the task.

AT 2: The variety of life (levels 5, 9)

'Pupils should make a more detailed and quantitative study of a locality . . . they should seek out and use reference materials in making this study and translate the information from one form to another in communicating it to a specific audience.'

AT 7: Making new materials (levels 4, 7)

'Pupils should have the opportunities to research the manufacturing process involved in . . . the production of fertilizers and to relate this research to experimental methods used in the school laboratory.

'Pupils should explore the social, economic, environmental and health and safety implications of manufacture, including the effects of changing economic conditions on the suitability of particular processes.'

AT 17: The nature of science (levels 4-10)

'Focused on the life and work of a famous scientist and/or the development of an important idea in science, pupils should be given opportunities to consider how the development relates to its historical and cultural — including the spiritual and moral — context.'

In planning the drama and science work, some basic questions need to be addressed:

Where will the drama take place?
Who is to lead the drama work within the lesson?
What information will be needed by the teacher? by the pupil?
How will the pupils' information be gained?
What information sources will be provided by the teacher? How much will the pupils be expected to research for themselves?
At what point will the science and drama interact? How? Where?
Is the aim of the work a presentation of some kind? If so, who is the identified audience?

Activity 1: Using the still image

In order to appreciate Haber's position in German society of the time, pupils will need to consider first an oppressed, isolated group of whom they might have some knowledge or experience.

Ask pupils in pairs to identify between them any groups who are in this position. Try not to give them the ideas. Ask those pairs (or threes, if odd numbers) to join with another and share the groups they have identified, and settle on one choice to bring back to the whole group. Ask for this group's identity to be written on a large label, and for all the labels to be placed simultaneously on the floor for all to see. Discuss the groups with the class. Are there any important omissions?

Ask pupils, now in groups of four or five, to make a still picture/image/tableau of a scene which will represent the group they have identified. Give about 10 minutes for this. Ask groups to show their images to one another and encourage respectful consideration of their efforts. Can they identify a message? Is there a word or phrase which labels them? Put their suggestions — *all* of them — on the blackboard or preferably a large sheet of paper; you or they may want to go back to these offerings later.

Introduce a short piece describing Jewish life — it does not have to be in Germany but there are numerous examples in literature. A passage from *The Diary of Anne Frank* might be used. Discuss the feelings being expressed again; ask pupils to offer them aloud for recording on a large sheet. Compare the two. A carefully chosen piece will stimulate much in common with the first list.

Activity 2: 'A day in the life'

In order to create a context, ask pupils as a whole class to identify scenes that might have occurred in a day in Haber's life as a child or young teenager (with the teacher helping discussion). He was clearly gifted and Jewish, so family and school would be the focus for these scenes. This could raise questions such as 'how are gifted people treated by their family, friends, schoolfellows, teachers?'. Within his family he would be valued, encouraged, praised, but outside the family he might have encountered abuse because of his religion and his ability. There may be a need for research here into the Jewish religion — perhaps tying up with religious education studies for help regarding the way in which a young male would have been treated in a Jewish household.

Ask pupils to identify, with some guidance, perhaps five or six scenes.

e.g. early morning at home — the family at breakfast
before class begins — discussing work

lesson in progress
returning home from school
at dinner in the evening with the family

The groups created at the end of activity 1 can be used again. By creating these short scenes in small groups pupils will begin to identify with Haber as a young teenager and the difficulties he faced then. How he deals with them is their decision. In presenting the scenes to the rest of the class after approximately 20 minutes of preparation time, allowance must be given for pupils to respond to what they have seen. Does it fit their view of Haber? What kind of person do they think he was? How did his early experiences prepare him for what was to come?

Activity 3: The Nobel prizewinner

Haber won the Nobel Prize for Chemistry in 1918, ten years after he had developed his ammonia process in the laboratory, during which time he had seen a process developed to feed the world also used to provide the raw material to destroy it.

Had Germany not had the ability to produce nitrogen chemically, the First World War would certainly have ended before 1918, owing to Germany's lack of food and explosives.

The whole class here will be involved in speaking aloud the thoughts of Haber and of Bosch, the man who developed the industrial plant from Haber's original process.

Imagine a meeting between the two men immediately following the prize-giving. Ask two pupils to volunteer to represent them in the action of a handshake of congratulation. As the two shake hands, freeze the action and ask the class, divided in half, to say aloud anything they think their 'person' might be thinking at that moment. Encourage them to offer ideas freely; do not ask around a circle in order, this will intimidate rather than encourage. Some will give many ideas, some may repeat what others say, some may say nothing, only listen to the responses of others. Listen first to one person's 'thoughts' then to the other.

After this ask the two 'actors' which thoughts they felt were the most appropriate to them. Were there any that were not appropriate? Encourage the rest of the class to assess their thoughts and those of the other person.

Here is the root of moral dilemma; this activity should lead to a greater awareness of the choices people are faced with, and how they deal with them.

Another context for this activity would be the handshake sealing the sale of Haber's rights to his ammonia process to BASF, a leading German chemical company. The two people would then be Haber and the managing director of the company. This meeting would stimulate financial and political comment perhaps more obviously than the one above.

Activity 4: The teacher in role

Haber ended his life in a mental hospital, torn apart by the anguish created by the dual use of his original ammonia process and also because he had become an embarrassment to the 'authorities'. What did Haber feel about his life and work?

In this activity the teacher plays the part of Haber. The class, as themselves, question him as they see fit about his life, his opinions, his work, other people, whatever they feel they wish to know. This means the teacher must have some knowledge of the man and his work.

This is a very stimulating way of informing pupils, which they remember and respond well to. The teacher needs to be creative if questions are about feelings, but must try to be true to the 'spirit' of the person. At the end of the activity, with teacher back in role as teacher, ask pupils if they were happy with the responses. Did they disagree with any of the responses and if so, why?

Activity 5: The chemical process

Earlier in the chapter, the idea of pupils acting out the chemical activity, taking the parts of molecules in the process or of conditions which affect them, was mentioned as an effective way of helping pupils to understand the stages in a process. The Haber process is a good example of this. Pupils are able to role play through the process. Labelling can be done very simply using coloured badges or signs of the elements involved and labels for such things as a heat exchanger or a catalytic converter. The elements involved are encouraged to move through the different processes, re-forming as the changes occur. The whole idea can be reworked with pupils taking on the roles of different elements and processes.

These five activities are used as illustration of method. They can be reworked in many different guises, used individually or as a whole package to stimulate and encourage pupils into discussion. If desired, the package could form the basis of improvisation work leading to performance, but this would require much more intensive work on the drama.

The ideas offered could all be handled within the science classroom, though several might be more comfortably tackled in a more open space such as a small hall or drama studio. Interwoven with the science-specific work, the ideas should draw pupils into a greater awareness of Haber as a person and the choices he faced, the difficulties of a scientist in a commercial world and how problematic the role can be.

There are other scientists whose work can be looked at in this way, though it is to be hoped that teachers will have been stimulated to look beyond this one specific area to other aspects of the science curriculum which have potential for a drama approach. For the potential is enormous. Once drama and science teachers begin to look for material which will lend itself to a dramatic method there are few Attainment Targets which would not be enlivened by the use of the techniques.

Teacher talking to teacher about the learning experience and how to enrich it for all pupils is the starting point. That the science teacher and the drama teacher can work together is certain, that their pupils can benefit in many ways is unquestionable, that each subject area can benefit is assured. So, let the dialogue begin.

REFERENCES

HMI [Her Majesty's Inspectorate] (1989) *Curriculum Matters 17: Drama from 5 to 16.* London: HMI.

NCC [National Curriculum Council] (1900) Arts in Schools Project.

NCC [National Curriculum Council] (1989) *Science: Non-Statutory Guidance.* York: National Curriculum Council.

Chapter 7

Science: The Person

Di Bentley

> The greenhouse effect means the earth is getting hotter, because we're using too many cars and too much petrol.
>
> (Kelly, aged 8)

> I think more people should walk. Lots of children come to my school every day in the car, but they live close. If we used cars less there might be less greenhouse effect.
>
> (Jonathon, aged 10)

> I think the ozone layer is a sort of layer of cloud very high above the earth. It protects us from the sun and stops us getting burnt up. But we've made holes in it so it protects us less now. . . . I'm not sure what will happen if it goes away altogether. I expect we'll have droughts and not much will grow. It will be like a desert. More people will probably get skin cancer.
>
> (Sanjiv, aged 12)

> I don't really know what causes AIDS. I know they're finding it difficult to find a cure, and that for me and my friends, it's made us think about relationships a bit differently — from how my mother did. My mum says she's glad AIDS wasn't around in her day!
>
> (Debbie, aged 16)

This chapter could be described as being about the spaces in the science curriculum. For between the warp of the profile component of *knowledge and understanding*, and the weft of the *exploration of science*, lie the holes that are the *'cross-curricular themes'*: those parts of the curriculum that reach the parts that others cannot reach — the bits everyone knows are important and that are usually described as 'bringing relevance' or 'providing contexts' or 'exploring applications'. All of these descriptions are apt, as far as science is concerned, for the cross-curricular themes do provide the opportunity for exploring scientific concepts in real contexts that are directly related to the important aspects of everyday life. In this chapter I explore ways of ensuring that cross-curricular themes, in particular those of health and environmental education, are taken into account when planning for the National Curriculum and its delivery, in both profile components.

The first point to establish is that we are not talking about anything new. As the quotes which open the chapter show, the knowledge is there in our youngsters, as society becomes more concerned about the global problems facing it. The interrelationships of human beings, their societal, physical and biological environments, are a part of the understanding of students. When these four future citizens were asked where they learned about issues of the environment, they quoted newspapers and the television as often as they quoted school. Sanjiv and Debbie are too old now to benefit from the National Curriculum. Kelly and Jonathon, when asked in three or four years' time (in the middle of their programmes of study for key stage 3) how they know about environmental issues, will be able to quote school as a major influence on their learning.

CROSS-CURRICULAR THEMES AND DIMENSIONS

There are five cross-curricular themes designated by the National Curriculum Council (NCC):

Economic and industrial understanding
Education for citizenship
Careers education and guidance
Health education
Environmental education

Circular Number 6 (NCC, 1988) states that the cross-curricular themes must be regarded as part of every student's entitlement to a whole curriculum:

> The cross curricular themes contribute to personal and social development in a number of ways:
> 1. They explore the values and beliefs which influence the individual and his or her relationship with others and the wider world.

2. They help pupils to respond to their present lives and prepare them for work and adult life
3. They emphasise practical activities, decision making, learning through experience and the development of close links between the school and the wider world.
4. They provide relevant ways in which skills might be developed.
(NCC, 1988 para. 17)

I would go further. In the case of environmental and health education, I would say that these themes should also provide essential knowledge without which the development of an individual, and that of local and global communities, will be much reduced. Much of that knowledge depends on an understanding of some basic scientific concepts. Within the National Curriculum, science has a responsibility to young citizens like Jonathon and Kelly. It has the responsibility to help them understand the concepts and make the link between these concepts and the issues of health and the environment. The statements from the NCC provide a clear indication of the kinds of teaching and learning strategies which might be required to implement the cross-curricular themes. These include those that encourage:

learning through direct experience
exploring beliefs and values
decision making
practical activities
linking with home and the community
skill development
exploring opinions

Later in the chapter I provide examples of how such approaches might be mapped and carried out.

There is no doubt, too, that the cross-curricular themes provide opportunities for a variety of models of cooperation between different departments in a secondary school that were never there before in quite such an explicit way. Within the subject basis of the National Curriculum itself, the geography report (DES and Welsh Office, 1990a) and technology Standing Orders (DES and Welsh Office, 1990b) also give examples of places where cooperation and possibly thematic development might occur.

The other aspects of the whole curriculum that have a direct bearing on the 'person and the environment' are the *cross-curricular dimensions.* These are intended to permeate many aspects of teaching the National Curriculum subjects. The NCC has designated three of these:

personal and social development
equal opportunities
multicultural education

The last two are the subject of Chapter 8, but I shall attempt to deal with some of the issues of the first as it impinges on health education in the second part of this chapter.

ENVIRONMENTAL EDUCATION

There is no shortage of advice and guidance on environmental issues within and around the National Curriculum. The NCC, through standing orders, non-statutory guidance and cross-curricular working party reports, seems determined that all teachers, and science teachers in particular, should not forget the environmental agenda. Indeed there is such a plethora of suggestions and advice that the difficult task is to sort through it all to be sure that what is essential is being done, as well as what can reasonably be accomplished on top of this in an overcrowded work schedule.

Some of the links between science and the environment are obvious in the programmes of study for science. For example, 16 of the original 20 statements of attainment in the levels of Attainment Target 5 are concerned with the environment. The programmes of study for each of the key stages outline aspects of the environment which need to be taught:

Key stage 3
[pupils] should be given the opportunity to study how science is applied in a variety of contexts. . . . They should consider the advantages and drawbacks of applying scientific and technological ideas to themselves, industry, the environment and the community. They should begin to make personal decisions and judgements based upon their scientific knowledge of issues concerning personal health and well being, safety and the care of the environment.

Key stage 4
[pupils] should use their science knowledge and skills to make decisions and judgements and consider the effect of scientific and

technological developments on individuals, communities and environments. Through this study, they should begin to understand the power and limitations of science in solving, industrial, social, and environmental problems and recognise the competing priorities and risks involved.

(DES and Welsh Office, 1989)

Although these are obvious features mainly concerned with knowledge and understanding — many of them appearing in Attainment Target 5 — it is also important to consider other Attainment Targets where issues of the environment may be less obvious but can also play a part and to be sure what aspects of environmental education we wish to encourage. The advice on cross-curricular themes given earlier indicates some skills and teaching approaches which are important. However, the NCC working party on the cross-curricular theme of environmental education has gone further than these generalizations. It has suggested an environmental charter for students as part of their entitlement to a whole curriculum.

An environmental charter

By the age of 16, all pupils should have had educational experience, related to local and global contexts which enables them to:

- Understand the natural processes which take place in the environment, including ecological principles and relationships.
- Understand that human lives and livelihoods are dependent upon the processes, inter-relationships and resources that exist in the environment.
- Be aware of the impact of human activities on the environment, including planning and design; understand the processes by which communities organise themselves, initiate and cope with change; appreciate that these processes are affected by a range of considerations (personal, economic, technological, social, aesthetic, political, cultural, ethical and spiritual).
- Be competent in a range of skills which help them to appreciate and enjoy the environment, communicate ideas, and participate in the decision making processes which shape the environment.
- View, evaluate and interpret and experience their surroundings critically.
- Have insights into a range of environments and cultures, both past and present and appreciate the ways in which different cultural groups perceive and interact with their environment.
- Understand the conflicts that may arise over environmental

issues, particularly in relation to the use of resources and consider a variety of ways in which to resolve such conflicts.
- Be aware that the current state of the environment has resulted from past decisions and actions and that the future of the environment depends on contemporary decisions and actions to which pupils can and will make a contribution.
- Form reasoned opinions on the basis of scientific evidence and develop informed balanced judgements regarding environmental issues and identify their own level of commitment towards the care of the environment.

(NCC, 1990b)

Not to be outdone, the NCC non-statutory guidance (NCC, 1989) has also drawn the attention of teachers to attitudes that should be fostered. They include:

- curiosity
- respect for evidence
- willingness to tolerate uncertainty
- critical reflection
- perseverance
- creativity and inventiveness
- open-mindedness
- sensitivity to the living and non-living environment
- cooperation with others.

With all this advice, how is it possible to sort out what to teach? Some useful and simple categories are provided by work done by the Association for Science Education (ASE). These cut across the advice outlined earlier and make it more manageable when planning schemes of work and links with other colleagues.

Opening Doors for Science (ASE/NCC, 1990) states that

Environmental education through science aims to help pupils to develop and apply science knowledge and skills to make decisions in order to prevent or solve problems concerned with caring for the whole environment. This should be based on their own or other people's scientific evidence.

It suggests three major contexts for environmental education through science:

1. Education *about* the environment. Concerned with developing knowledge about the content and processes of the environment.
2. Education *in* the environment. Learning science outside the

Table 7.1 *An analysis of the environmental education contexts for science in the National Curriculum*

Old Attainment Target	Key stages				Model B for key stage 4
	1	2	3	4	
1 Exploration of science	AIF	AIF	AIF	AIF	*
2 The variety of life	AIF	AIF	AIF	AIF	
3 Processes of life	–	A	–	A	*
4 Genetics and evolution	–	A	A	AF	*
5 Human influences on the Earth	AIF	AIF	AIF	AIF	
6 Types and uses of materials	AI	A	–	AF	*
7 Making new materials			A	A	
8 Explaining how materials behave			AF	–	*
9 Earth and atmosphere	AI	AI	AI	AI	*
10 Forces	–	A	A	A	*
11 Electricity and magnetism	–	–	A	AF	*
12 Information technology	–	AI	AI	–	
13 Energy	–	AF	AF	AF	*
14 Sound and music	–	–	AF	–	*
15 Using light and electromagnetic radiation	AI	–	–	–	
16 The Earth in space	AI	AI	A	A	
17 The nature of science			AF	AF	

In the text there are *specific* statements of science:
A – About the environment
I – In the environment
F – For the environment
Source: adapted from ASE/NCC (1990, p. 11)

classroom, in the real context for scientific understanding.
3. Education *for* the environment. Concerned with enabling students to form opinions and make decisions about the links between human activity and the environment. This is a challenging part of science education and the most vital context for environmental education. (Adapted from ASE/NCC, 1990, pp. 5–6)

Table 7.1 indicates where each of the three contexts occurs in the original Attainment Targets. It has been derived from an analysis of the statements of attainment.

So how can we achieve the impossible? One clear first step is careful planning. Figures 7.1 and 7.2 show a first step that any science department might take in this process. They represent what secondary teachers call a concept map, and primary teachers a topic web. Both figures represent a brainstorm of activities that could be included in schemes of work. Figure 7.1 focuses on Old Attainment Target 5 (Human Influences on the Earth) and directs itself at 12-year-old students (second-years). Figure 7.2 is intended to be for students in key stage 4 and focuses on the less obvious Attainment Target 6: 'Types and Uses of Materials'.

Once the concept maps have been established, it is important to focus them into a scheme of work by looking at the various categories identified in the advice quoted earlier. Checklists 1 and

---

CHECKLIST 1
ISSUES FOR INCLUDING IN TEACHING—
Fulfilling the environmental charter   **Activity**

Are there activities which help students to:

— understand natural environmental processes
— be aware of the impact of human activities
— appreciate that processes are affected by a range of considerations:

personal
economic
technological
social
aesthetic
political
cultural
ethical
spiritual

— have insights into a range of environments and cultures, and how they interact with their environment
— understand the conflicts that may arise over the use of resources and consider a variety of ways in which to resolve such conflicts
— be aware that the current state of the environment has resulted from past decisions and actions
— form reasoned opinions on the basis of scientific evidence
— develop informed, balanced judgements on environmental issues
— identify their own level of commitment to the care of the environment.

CHECKLIST 2
TEACHING APPROACHES, SKILLS AND ATTITUDES
Activities

Teaching approaches

Learning through direct experience
Exploring opinions, beliefs and values
Decision making
Practical activities
Linking with home and the community
Skill development
Work in the environment
Problem solving

Skills

Applying scientific and technological ideas
Making personal decisions and judgements based on scientific knowledge
Understanding the power and limitations of science
Solving problems
Planning
Designing
Communicating ideas
Evaluating
Experiencing surroundings critically

Attitudes

Curiosity
Respect for evidence
Willingness to tolerate uncertainty
Critical reflection
Perseverance
Creativity and inventiveness
Open-mindedness
Sensitivity to the living and non-living environment
Cooperation with others.

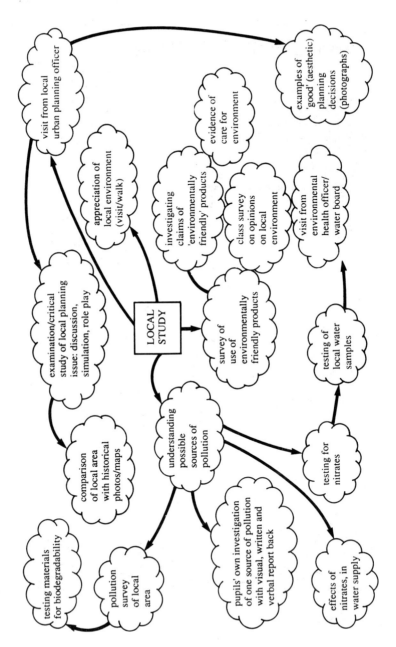

Figure 7.1 Key stage 3, Attainment Target 5, concept/activity map

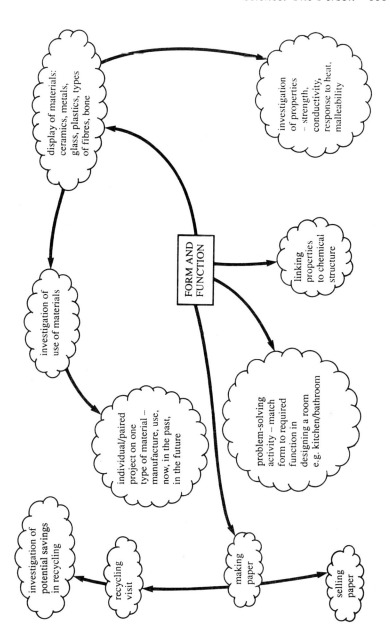

Figure 7.2 Key stage 4, Attainment Target 6, concept/activity map

2 may help; they are designed to be used for long-term planning over a key stage. It is not expected that all the aspects in, for example, the environmental charter would be included in every unit or module of work.

For those seeking more detail of how to carry out some of these activities, the case studies in *Opening Doors for Science* (ASE/NCC, 1990) provide a rich source of ideas.

HEALTH EDUCATION

As with environmental education, there are some very obvious links between health and science education in the National Curriculum. The appendix to *Curriculum Guidance Five* (NCC, 1990a) outlines these for each of the key stages in science. It is clear that many of them arise from Old Attainment Targets 3 and 4, but also included are issues of energy (AT 13), forces (AT 10), sound (AT 14), electricity (AT 11) and, of course, aspects of health arising from AT 17. Although some of these links are obvious, it is important first of all to establish exactly what we mean by health and, given that it is a cross-curricular theme, what contribution science has to make to the whole. Definitions of health education abound, but most of them include reference to the consideration of physical, social and emotional aspects of life. The NCC for example states that:

> Essential features of health education are the promotion of quality of life and the physical, social and mental well being of the individual. It covers the provision of information about what is good and what is harmful and involves the development of skills which will help individuals to use their knowledge effectively.
>
> (NCC, 1990a)

As science teachers, we need to consider whether science should try to provide a particular focus within these—for example the physical aspects, leaving social and emotional areas to other subjects. My personal opinion is that this is not possible. If we are to assist students to make decisions about their own health-related behaviour, in full knowledge of the risks associated with particular types of behaviour, we need to help them learn to take into account the social aspects of such behaviour. After all, they will not be making their future decisions in some clinical environment divorced from emotions and social pressures. Science can assist this decision-making process by making the following three major contributions:

> help young people develop competence in the use of scientific ideas
> . . . [so that] they become an effective basis for positive action and
> . . . help youngsters develop competence in the skills of relationships,
> analysing, inferring and decision making.
> . . . enable young people to explore the limitations of scientific
> knowledge as an exemplification of the human condition.
>
> (SSCR, 1987, p. 12)

The NCC (1990a) suggests nine curriculum components for a health education programme, with aspects which emphasize the interest of the individual, the group (such as families or particular professions) and the community. The curriculum areas are:

- Substance use and misuse
- Sex education
- Family life education
- Safety
- Health-related exercise
- Food and nutrition
- Personal hygiene
- Environmental aspects of health education
- Psychological aspects of health education

There are obvious links between science and this list. With the exception of the third and the last, most science teachers would recognize these items as having been an integral part of the science curriculum for years. Nor has the situation altered greatly with the National Curriculum. In 1989 the NCC suggested that AT 1 (Exploration of Science), not surprisingly, should be involved in all of the nine areas. Of the other Attainment Targets, AT 3 (Processes of Life) has something to contribute to all areas, while ATs 6, 9 and 12 (respectively Types and Uses of Materials, Earth and Atmosphere, and Information Technology) have much less if anything at all. In a strict sense, this is probably true of AT 12, but the use of a computer to collect data on health and fitness, for example, can provide a real and important context for teaching in this area. There are now a wide range of products on the market which capture such data and allow students to analyse it, compare it with their own previous figures or with class and other norms.

But knowledge and understanding of issues is merely one small part of health education. The NCC has stressed that AT 1 is integral to all health education. If we re-examine the programmes of study within AT 1 from a health perspective, they might look something like the example in Figure 7.3.

Yet this does not really portray the essential feature of health education; that is, the skill of decision making. To some extent it can be found in AT 1, as the example in Figure 7.3 shows, but it is not the major purpose of this Attainment Target, whereas it is crucial to health education. In failing to explore this aspect fully the NCC

KEY STAGE 3

Pupils should:

be able to analyse data relating to health issues presented in a variety of simple written and pictorial forms;

use health concepts to formulate hypotheses about the interrelationships of health information and their own lifestyles;

be able to comment critically on health-related material;

support an opinion on health-related matters by reference to data;

make decisions about the effects of particular behaviours on their own personal health;

offer ideas and take initiative in groups;

be able to confront conflicting opinions in a group without the group breaking up.

KEY STAGE 4

Pupils should:

evaluate conflicting arguments about health-related issues;

know how to distinguish between fact, promotion and polemic in health-related areas;

know how to weigh and interpret information and evidence about health from a variety of sources;

be able to make informed judgements about the relationship between social, economic and personal factors and the health of individuals;

be able to make informed choices about their own health-related behaviour;

modify their own ideas in the light of those of others in their group;

help in the effective management of resources in a group enterprise;

take on different roles in a group as determined by the task;

see a group task through to completion.

Figure 7.3

cross-curricular working party missed a real opportunity to develop something very exciting in health education. Providing real examples of how teachers might use health information and practical experimentation to teach decision-making skills would have been a major step forward. Instead, the working party devoted a great deal of space to a list of content, much of which was already self-evident in different standing orders.

Like problem solving, decision making has aspects that need to be taught explicitly. Effective health education relies on assisting students to find their way through a maze of often contradictory information, relate it to the way they want to live their lives and take decisions for action accordingly.

Fortunately, before the NCC came into existence a large number of health educationists had recognized this and produced a great variety of materials to serve the need. Admittedly, these need careful study, for two reasons. First, they were written before anyone had heard of Attainment Targets and so their match with the National Curriculum is not firm. Secondly, few if any were written by scientists with science in mind. This is both a bonus and a difficulty. The major thrust of these materials is often to encourage decision making on health issues in a fully cross-curricular way. As they are decontextualized from any subject association they contain teaching approaches which may not be a common feature of many science lessons. Although some teachers may find this a problem at first, they should persevere.

Teaching approaches

One of the most important aspects of teaching health and environmental education is the consideration not of *what* to teach but of *how* to teach it. The NCC suggests that a range of learning opportunities should be available to students, which include assessing evidence, solving problems, decision making and discussions. All these opportunities have implications for the teaching approaches that teachers choose and their management of the classroom environment. The different teaching approaches available to science teachers cannot possibly be given due consideration in the space of this chapter; readers can find much more information in texts such as *Better Science* (SSCR, 1987a, b), *Learning and Teaching in*

CHECKLIST 3 LEARNING OPPORTUNITIES

Assessing evidence
Making decisions
Negotiating
Listening
Making relationships
Dealing with relationships
Solving problems
Working independently
Working confidently

School Science (Bentley and Watts, 1989) and a variety of TACADE publications (e.g. TACADE, 1985). However, in planning inclusion of cross-curricular themes there is no doubt that some teaching approaches lend themselves best to particular types of skill development. It may assist readers to have checklists (above and opposite) of the NCC learning opportunities and a range of teaching approaches which they can use when writing schemes and planning activities.

Health education, like all cross-curricular themes, provides a context for teaching science in which scientific knowledge can be put to use to make decisions which will be crucial to students at some point in their lives. The interrelation of scientific understanding and personal decision making is crucial: one cannot be successful without the other. The knowledge is not sufficient alone. Science teachers cannot assume that teaching the scientific concepts is to be their only contribution; they have a responsibility to help students use them to make inferences and judgements. The contextualizing of scientific examples in a health or environmental example is essential if students are to have the opportunity to practise decision making. So too is providing the learning experiences and environment within which that decision making can prosper.

ADVICE FOR SCIENCE DEPARTMENTS

In its guidance on health education, the NCC suggests that there are at least six ways in which the teaching of health education can be

---

CHECKLIST 4 TEACHING APPROACHES

Project work
Discussion
Small-group work
Audio-visual work
Community visits
Case studies
Problem solving
Decision making
Self-directed learning
Role playing
Simulation
Games
Questionnaires
Surveys
Value clarification

---

managed across the curriculum, and provides the pros and cons of each approach. These are obviously important considerations for the whole school. However, there is no denying that all schools will teach science to all students, or that health and environmentally related issues are actually written into the National Curriculum for science — overtly in the case of some Attainment Targets. So whatever decision is made by the school concerning the management of its cross-curricular themes, science teachers will have to cover aspects of health and environmental education. What can a science department do to ensure that the cross-curricular themes are being included in its work or, more importantly, that the science department contributes to cross-curricular work in the school in a meaningful way? There are some fairly straightforward steps.

Conducting a curriculum audit

Using the checklists provided in this chapter, the department could look through the existing schemes of work and identify where the skills, attitudes and information are being taught at present, where the gaps are and how these might best be filled. One interesting approach to this in environmental education is to use the ASE working party criteria of education *about*, *in* and *for* the environment. A common finding in such audits is that education about the environment is common, education in the environment less so (often because of cost), and education for the environment fairly infrequent, since it involves teaching approaches which are time consuming and often seen as 'not real science'. Yet, as the section on health education shows, this need not be the case. Several of the statements of attainment in AT 1 can be achieved by careful examination of a variety of evidence, which can also lead to enhancement in decision-making skills, evaluating, inferring and so on — all part of the aspects which the cross-curricular themes require.

A curriculum audit need not be one that simply focuses on present practice. It may refocus attention on the programmes of study. The checklists can be used to re-examine the programmes of study from a cross-curricular viewpoint, and to plan new activities that will provide the necessary experiences. Such an audit could form the basis for a revision of existing schemes of work in an attempt to emphasize cross-curricular themes.

Conducting a resource audit

No curriculum audit is complete without a matching resource audit. There are four aspects to this.

Materials

Existing materials need careful examination. In an area of the curriculum where newspapers, books and television are a continual source of ideas, and textbooks are often out of date, a regular review of the relevance of existing materials needs to take place. Any such review also needs to include 'balance and bias' checks. Ask questions such as:

- does the material contain a range of opinions so that students' skills in decision making are enhanced?
- what view of other cultures does material based on global issues present? Is it a positive or a potentially racist one?

- has the view of other cultures about their situation been explored? (The views of Brazilians on the burning of their rain forests are a good example here.)

Reviewing materials in this way against a set of carefully agreed and chosen criteria is a very useful exercise to conduct with the students. It serves two purposes: it does the work in half the time, and it assists in sharpening students' skills of critical analysis. The review could well be a simple group exercise that students are asked to conduct every time they use materials in the course of their work. Completing an evaluation tick sheet which is stored and then re-examined once a year is a quick method of identifying which materials require revision.

Equipment

Just as any stock is reviewed on a regular basis, so equipment needs to be reviewed for the specialist purpose which it serves. Some items which assist in the scientific exploration of evidence about health and the environment are expensive. They may or may not be essential. In either case it is worth making an analysis of what is available to support each of the teaching approaches and activities planned. A whole-school approach to this may inform many staff about expensive and little-used equipment that could enhance their teaching and so prove cost-effective.

Expertise

It has become very clear that there are some areas of the National Curriculum in which science teachers are extremely skilled and some where knowledge and skills need updating or developing. Identifying individuals in the department and whole school who are interested in cross-curricular issues, who have good practice to share — particularly in the less well known teaching approaches — or who would be prepared to have more INSET on behalf of the department, bringing those skills back to assist others, is a crucial part of any audit.

Finance

Education in the environment can be an expensive business; it needs careful planning within the curriculum if the maximum benefit is to be gained from it. Purchase of expensive items of equipment also needs careful planning. All such financial considerations, in the era of LMS when many departments have a budget to manage and account for, need thought. Decisions may have to be made about seeking extra funding to support some developments. These aspects require decision making by the whole department.

So far I have discussed cross-curricular themes as though they are involved only in the science department. Clearly, by definition, they involve most other departments in the school. So an essential step, once audits have been conducted to ascertain the state of the *science* department, is to engage in dialogues with others.

Working with other departments

In most schools there are many avenues and forums for working with other departments. Heads of department meetings are an obvious place. Some schools have set up cross-curricular working parties to conduct whole-school audits of the type described above. Other suggestions might include:

- a science open evening for staff—sharing schemes of work, students' work, and teaching approaches to allow other staff to see where the connections might lie.
- a science open department meeting—an open discussion, to which any other members of staff may come, which focuses on links with others. A useful time to do this is when the results of the 'brewing unit' come to fruition!
- a resource fair—sharing resources with other departments to see what is available that might conceivably be borrowed or used collectively.
- an expertise fair—where staff members share their favourite teaching approach with other members of staff from other subjects—centred around a theme, for example.

These fairly low-key suggestions can result in awareness-raising about science and areas of the curriculum. What they do not necessarily do is bring about change. A drawback is that they may create an impression that the science department thinks it has all the answers, so that joining with another department in putting on 'fairs' would be a helpful approach. But change itself may need more than this.

Development planning

Although the above steps suggest examining the science department first, development planning is best begun in conjunction with other departments. There are essential first decisions to take about the nature and extent of cooperation between departments. In other words, is change to be radical — even if long term — or is it to be just cooperation, leaving the essential curriculum of the contributing departments unchanged?

Some cooperative suggestions

Cross-curricular work can be at a level of agreed resource sharing, so that the issues of expenditure are catered for and money is not wasted. It ensures that, for example, students do not see the same film/video twice in a year (week?!) in different subjects. This is what I would describe as a minimalist approach.

Another minimalist approach is temporal agreement: departments agree when in the year particular work is to be tackled. Films, visits and visitors are planned in a coordinated way so that students can draw experiences for science, geography, history and English from a common set of approaches. The teaching and aims of the individual departments remain unchanged. This avoids duplication and saves time.

Event planning: a visit or piece of fieldwork is the best example of this. Several departments use an expensive event such as a field trip around which to plan cooperatively. The field trip needs to be a thematic one which involves the skills required by each of the contributing departments. The substance of the knowledge being taught in the departments may be quite different; the field trip is what brings it together. So, for example, a field trip may be planned to a coastal area. Geographers would use it to examine issues about the coastline, scientists would develop a chemical trail showing corrosion, historians an examination of the change in occupations and/or housing style. The planning of the trip must be cooperative, the staff taking part need to understand sufficient of each other's area to help and support the students on the trip, and work leading up to it also needs to be planned carefully.

Some radical suggestions

Planning by cooperation   One department agrees to teach the theme on behalf of all the others. Resources are drawn from all contributing areas, expertise is used to construct materials and teaching situations, but one department is responsible for handling and organizing the whole theme. This may mean teaching outside one's specialism. It certainly requires that other departments do not duplicate this work, so they need to delete it from their curriculum. They also need to remind students that, for example, the skills they are learning in geography fieldwork are applicable in science too.

Planning by collaboration   The collaborating departments – for example geography, history, science, English, technology (home economics) – conduct curriculum audits. They choose an area where most conjunction of skills is possible and agree a theme for teaching the Attainment Targets associated with this theme in each of the areas of the curriculum. Resources are pooled, joint writing of materials takes place, plans are made to teach the theme across all the departments at the same time and teachers team-teach certain aspects where room proximity permits. (The planning cycle is such that the timetable can be constructed to allow team teaching to happen.) Students are informed before the theme begins that it is a cooperative effort – assembly can be used for this, and to introduce the issues involved in the theme – and the organization and expected end products are shared with them.

Planning resources

Cooperation in long-term planning for sharing resources and equipment may be useful. If departments have their own budgets they may be able to agree development options with other departments for the purchase of expensive equipment over a long timescale. Sharing expertise may be useful too. Having a member of the geography department attend an INSET course on environmental themes on behalf of science and geography can be a valuable way of distributing INSET monies, as can shared purchase of technician time, now that LMS allows the flexibility to do this. Planning staff development jointly is useful; for example, over a period of time one member of a department may develop skills in teaching lower-school science and technology, and will then be an asset to both departments, often assisting in solving staffing problems.

More adventurous methods of resource planning lie in developing cluster arrangements with other schools. An example is the buying of technician time, or buying in extra teacher support with INSET funds, so that the teacher is shared between several schools and works alongside colleagues in the classroom to enhance their skills.

The days of isolation are over. The National Curriculum places a requirement for cooperation and planning on teachers that is far in excess of anything that has taken place before. Primary colleagues are planning their work in teams and groups much more frequently. Secondary colleagues need to have a wider vision simply because their group is a larger one. Departmental planning is no longer sufficient; whole school is the way of the future, and collaboration is its password.

REFERENCES

ASE/NCC [Association for Science Education/Nature Conservancy Council] (1990) *Opening doors for Science*. Hatfield: Association for Science Education.

Bentley, D. and Watts, D. M. (1989) *Learning and Teaching in School Science: Practical Alternatives*. Milton Keynes: Open University Press.

DES [Department of Education and Science] and the Welsh Office (1989) *Science in the National Curriculum*. London: HMSO.

DES [Department of Education and Science] and the Welsh Office (1990a) *Geography for Ages 5 to 16. Proposals of the Secretary of State for Education and Science and the Secretary of State for Wales*. London: HMSO (June).

DES [Department of Education and Science] and Welsh Office (1990b) *Technology in the National Curriculum*. London: HMSO.

NCC [National Curriculum Council] (1988) *Circular Number 6.* York: NCC.

NCC [National Curriculum Council] (1989) *Science in the National Curriculum: Non-Statutory Guidance.* York: NCC.

NCC [National Curriculum Council] (1990a) *Curriculum Guidance Five: Health Education.* York: NCC.

NCC [National Curriculum Council] (1990b) Draft report, National Curriculum Working Party on Environmental Education. Mimeograph, National Curriculum Council, 1990.

SSCR [Secondary Science Curriculum Review] (1987a) *Better Science: Approaches to Teaching and Learning.* London: Association for Science Education/Heinemann.

SSCR [Secondary Science Curriculum Review] (1987b) *Better Science: Health and Science Education.* London: Association for Science Education/Heinemann.

TACADE (1985) *Free to Choose: An Approach to Drug Education.* Manchester: Teachers' Advisory Council for Alcohol and Drug Education.

Chapter 8

Science and Equal Opportunities
Pauline Hoyle

The term 'equal opportunities' has been used in a variety of different ways. Everybody has their own definition and meaning. The National Curriculum documentation uses the term in several ways but without defining it clearly once. For the sake of this chapter we shall define equal opportunities as an approach to education which ensures that all learners fulfil their potential and have equal access to the curriculum offered and to the learning environment. This requires that some account is taken of the different starting points, ideas and experiences that every learner brings to the learning situation, and that provision is made for all learners to realize fully their potential within the learning situation. This means that the approach to what is taught, how it is taught, and the environment in which it is taught must be adapted so that it is accessible to each and every learner.

Within these terms it is necessary to consider what factors affect the learner as we try to achieve equal access to curriculum and learning environment. It is generally accepted that a learner's gender, cultural background, ethnic group and class are the more obvious factors which influence access to learning. Other factors may influence a pupil's aptitude to learn, including those which earn the learner labels such as 'special needs pupil', 'pupil with learning difficulty', 'statemented pupil', 'bilingual learner', or 'gifted pupil', to name but a few. Each title summarizes a learning need that the pupil manifests which may be caused by specific emotional, behavioural or learning needs that must be addressed if pupils are to fulfil their learning potential. An equal opportunities approach to science education must therefore ensure that *all* pupils have an access to the curriculum in which account is taken of the *needs* of all pupils.

Every institution has its own rules and ethos which may or may not be welcoming and which may make the environment more or less accessible to *all* learners. Sexism, racism, classism, ageism and attitudes to disability all need to be addressed by schools that purport to have an equal-opportunities approach to education. Such an approach should both influence and change the ethos of an institution to ensure that *all* learners have equality of opportunity of access to the curriculum.

NATIONAL CURRICULUM STATEMENTS

I turn to the National Curriculum documentation to see what guidelines and provisions have been made in the statutes to ensure equality of access for all. As a science educator, it is to *Science in the National Curriculum* (DES, 1989) that I first look for guidance. Within the statutory guidelines very little is openly addressed about the issues outlined above. Some reference is made to pupils with special educational needs and the conditions under which they can be exempt, temporarily or otherwise, from the National Curriculum. Other more oblique references are made in the general introductions to the programmes of study about 'the application and economic, social and technological implications of science' which could be considered as inroads into addressing issues of equal opportunity. These will be investigated later in the chapter.

Within *Science: Non-Statutory Guidance* (NCC, 1990) actual reference *is* made to the issues involved in equal opportunities although the term itself is not used or explained. For example section A7 'Teaching Science' para. 7.4–7.9 deals with the issues of a common, balanced curriculum and the effect of girls in science, ethnic and cultural diversity, the influence of other 'cultures' in science, and special educational needs.

OTHER NATIONAL CURRICULUM DOCUMENTS

Before dealing with each section of *Science: Non-Statutory Guidance* in detail and deciding how they can best be developed within the constraints of the National Curriculum, it is important to consider other National Curriculum documentation that refers to equal opportunities. The National Curriculum Council *Circular No. 6* (1989a) is about cross-curricular issues. It outlines three areas of consideration: cross-curricular dimensions, cross-curricular themes and cross-curricular skills. Equal opportunities is outlined as one of the cross-curricular dimensions, as is multicultural education. At the time of writing no further details on what is meant by this are available from NCC. Examples of cross-curricular themes are health education, environmental education, and economic and industrial understanding. Obviously all these contain areas that pertain to science education as outlined by the programmes of study in *Science in the National Curriculum* (DES, 1989).

Circular No. 6 makes it clear that the purpose of the cross-curricular issues is to help schools view the curriculum as a whole and not consider it as ten subject areas of unconnected elements. This is a welcome step and in terms of equal opportunities it might help ensure that all areas of the curriculum offer an approach that supports equality of opportunity.

Gender

Paragraph 7.5 of the non-statutory guidelines suggests that a common, balanced curriculum (balanced science) 'will help eliminate the problems of sex imbalance in the uptake of specific courses'. Yet it acknowledges that the low expectations of many girls, particularly in physical science, will remain. It suggests that 'design of courses, use of materials which avoid sex stereotyping, involving of girls' own perspectives on problems, issues and ideas may help increase the involvement of girls in physical science'. In many ways this acknowledgement only scratches the surface of what is really involved in ensuring equality of opportunities for women in science. Traditionally science has been a pursuit of white Western middle-class men, which has determined the nature of the scientific ethos. Some research and writing (Bentley and Watts, 1986) suggests that for science to become truly accessible to women both the content of science and the approaches used in teaching and learning need to change and develop to widen the approach to what counts 'as science' and to create a more personalized and humane view of science. The ramifications of this will be examined later in the chapter, but for now it is sufficient to say that National Curriculum documentation *flags* the problem rather than offering a viable solution.

Ethnicity and culture

Paragraph 7.6 of non-statutory guidance (NCC, 1990) notes that teachers need to take account of the cultural and ethnic diversity within the school population, and of society at large, and suggests that different ethnic groups may have different interpretations of the view of science presented in the statutory orders (DES, 1989). It suggests that teachers need to take account of this – another admirable comment, but again the documentation does not suggest how this might be done and fails to spell out what the authors mean by the terms 'ethnic' and 'cultural', and why different 'ethnic' groups but not different 'cultural' groups may take different views of science. This section also spells out the difficulty of language in science. It appears to consider that it is the specialized 'language' of science and 'language' of instructions that cause difficulties for pupils. Here it does make suggestions on how these difficulties can be addressed. But for a *real* equal-opportunities approach this needs fully developing so as to consider how language development is the role of every science teacher for *all* their pupils, particularly special needs and bilingual pupils.

Paragraph 7.7 emphasizes 'that the choice of learning context has a strong effect on pupils' performance and this applies particularly to ethnic minority pupils'. The importance of using pupils' own experience as a context for learning is suggested as a solution. This approach has long been used by people developing approaches to ensure equality of education. But the rest of the paragraph goes on to impress that 'ethnic and cultural bias' should be excluded from both learning and assessment tasks. This is in contrast to the statements about gender and it is generally accepted that, in reality, removing bias is only possible some of the time. A more positive approach is to use bias as a teaching point so that a particular bias is made obvious to both the teacher and learner. The paragraph also states that 'cultural diversity can be a positive influence on the richness of the curriculum, provided the teacher does not take a narrow view of "correctness", for example in a discussion on diet or alternative energy'. This relates very clearly to paragraph A4.5 of the science non-statutory guidelines (NCC, 1990), which points out 'the powerful but provisional nature of science knowledge and explanation'. Any approach to science education which suggests otherwise will fail not only to present science in its broader contextual perspective but will also help put pupils of many backgrounds in conflict with their own and other cultural and/or religious beliefs. An obvious example is the theory of evolution. For some pupils this theory is in direct conflict with their religious/cultural beliefs and may generate dissonance between home and school if it is not dealt with sensitively and presented as *an* explanation rather than *the* accepted theory.

People in science

In the same document, paragraph 7.8 points to the fact that 'people from all cultures are involved in scientific enterprise'. This is an important point and needs relating to the previous idea that different groups of people have different ways of explaining the world around them. This paragraph also suggests that it is important for contributions to science from different cultures to be noted and that 'science books and learning materials should include people from different ethnic minority groups working alongside others in achieving success in scientific work'. Again these are important points, but they lack understanding of the issues involved. Surely examples should emphasize women as well as men? Although it is becoming easier to obtain examples of historical contributions from Arabic and Islamic, Chinese and Indian science, many of the examples currently used from these countries tend to show 'appropriate or intermediate technology' (which might be described in the West as 'low-tech') rather than much-sought-after 'high-tech, modern-style technology', as it would be described in middle-class Western society. Pupils can be very derogatory about 'low-tech' examples and the countries and people depicted, especially if they are not given examples of low-tech being used in the West as well. People in developing countries do aspire to 'high-tech' science, and it is commonly present in many cities, if not in the more rural settings.

It is also important for pupils to understand some of the social, economic and political reasons why certain cultures or groups of people have at different times dominated the explanations commonly held about phenomena in the world and the solutions to problems. For example Western science grew rapidly in the fifteenth century when the ideas from the developed Arabic science were finally translated into Latin so that the 'New World scientists' of the time could benefit and develop the ideas.

An equal-opportunities approach that shows science in its social, economic, religious and political context is partly suggested in Old Attainment Target 17 of the National Curriculum. However, to become a positive approach to equal opportunities this needs to be expanded.

OAT 17

In the non-statutory guidance (NCC, 1990) teaching strategies for OAT 17 are expanded and paragraph 2.4 states that role play or simulation is considered useful. I fully support the usefulness of the strategy itself, but the suggestion that 'If the location is in a Third World country an interesting multicultural element will also be involved' is at best naive and at worst patronizing and a good example of tokenism. Nor would any approach which takes equality seriously talk about the 'Third World', which has a distinctively negative connotation. In discussing issues such as energy it is better to start from contexts or events known to at least some of the students. In a culturally and ethnically diverse class students will have experiences from a whole range of situations (including other countries) to bring to the discussion. In ethnically homogeneous classes pupils will still bring a range of experiences about their own environment to a lesson. These can be explored and built upon. But in unknown contexts (such as other countries other than the UK) it is essential that pupils be able to research the whole social, economic and political ramifications of the issue before they make decisions necessary for role-play activities.

The documentation of the National Curriculum does give us some inroads into developing approaches which will ensure equality of opportunity for all. But the National Curriculum neglects important statements about how science has been used to support certain racist and sexist assumptions. It does not challenge inequality openly (see

ASE, 1990) and so lacks clarity and direction in supporting an equal-opportunities approach.

USING THE NATIONAL CURRICULUM TO DEVELOP AN EQUAL-OPPORTUNITIES APPROACH

Defining terms

Before addressing the ways in which one can develop an approach to science education within the framework of the National Curriculum it is probably useful to define some of the terms not defined by the National Curriculum. For example the words 'cultural' and 'ethnic', or 'ethnicity', have been used but not defined.
  Hussey (1982) succinctly defines both terms.

> Ethnicity is the term used to denote the ideas of a group to which one belongs through self identification or identification by others. The skin colour, type of hair and physical features common to a group may be the means of identification. Some ethnic groups may be identified by language, e.g. Welsh, Poles; some by religion or country of origin, e.g. Cypriot, Scots, Sylhetis, Chinese; others by both language and region of country of origin, e.g. Greek Cypriot, Bengalis; yet others by religion, language and culture, e.g. Jews, Sikhs and Hindus.

He defines culture in the following way:

> A culture is a way of life and may encompass the notion of life-styles as well as that of high culture, i.e. that which is held by the dominant or educated groups to be a desirable pattern of life, or set of tenets by which one aspires to live. It may also include the ideas of social status that one achieves or hopes to achieve through education and/or socialisation. It is often, but not always determined by one's economic circumstances. It may also be associated with language or religion. For instance, it is possible for one to be English and lead an Islamic cultural life. . . . The concept is too broad and cultures too dynamic to be accurate as a means of classifying peoples. However, curricula may involve a selection from a culture or cultures and may therefore be aptly described as multi-cultural.

Both are useful as working definitions, since they allow me to draw a distinction between culture and ethnicity which is valuable in considering how education can work towards equality and justice. Culture is a broad term that encompasses many aspects of a person, including gender, class and social status, whereas ethnicity has a narrower definition.

All aspects of the culture and ethnicity of pupils need to be recognized, valued and used if they are truly to benefit from and have equality of access to education. How can this be achieved in science education as defined by the National Curriculum?

The nature of science

Of paramount importance are both the nature of the science presented to pupils and the way in which that science is presented. For instance, it is important for science to be presented as just one way of explaining the world around us. School science needs to show that science and scientists are not neutral but that their observations, theories and explanations are bound by all the aspects of society that surrounds them: by social mores, economic and political understanding, religious and moral convictions.

In many ways Attainment Targets 1 and 17 and their associated programmes of study do enable us to establish this approach to science. AT 17 does not mention the political influences on science (perhaps because it would be unacceptable to government sensitivities?). The weighting being given to AT 1 is an important guideline to the way in which science educators need to construct their curricula. One advantage of the National Curriculum is that it tells us what to teach, but not how. As already mentioned, it is the way in which the science is presented that is of vital importance in establishing equality of approach. If the science presented to pupils leads them to consider it as a 'body of knowledge' and understanding to be learned and regurgitated, with the occasional need to be creative and solve a few problems, it is unlikely that students will gain equality of access. Students may be involved in investigation and experimenting but then get the message that 'actually, kids, you have done quite well but here are the correct results. Do copy them down and learn them. Remember you'll become better scientists if you learn the right answers.' This message gives pupils a false picture of science. For further work in this area see Russell and Munby (1989).

An approach that works towards equality and justice would involve the pupils in investigation and experimentation, often starting from their own questions and ideas and working towards pupils' developing their own understanding of the issues. This may mean that at times pupils and teachers differ in their way of explaining the world around them. This may arise from different cultural or ethnic backgrounds or it may just show that pupils are at a particular stage in their understanding. However, the implications of assessment cannot be overlooked. This approach may allow pupils to achieve very well on parts of Attainment Targets 1 and 17 but not on the rest of profile component 2, Knowledge and Understanding. It is a difficult dilemma but perhaps can be resolved by letting pupils into the 'game' i.e. 'I agree with what you've done and found out, and I follow your conclusions, but it's only fair to warn you that not everybody agrees with you. I don't agree with you because . . . /or other scientists think that . . . what do you say to that?'

So the approach used in presenting science and the way in which ATs 1 and 17 are incorporated into the classwork give vital clues to the teacher's view on the nature of science and its role in describing the world. The views portrayed to the pupil will have powerful connotations, giving them messages about whether this is a view of the world to which they can have access, or whether it is an elite and alienating view inaccessible to them and contrary to their own 'world view'.

A WAY FORWARD

Context

It is the context in which science is presented that can often be the key to developing a equal-opportunities approach. The National Curriculum, as outlined both in the programmes of study and the statements of attainment, does not prescribe the mode of presentation. Creating an innovative setting is still left to teachers' creativity and ingenuity. It is worth examining several approaches to curriculum development that different people have used in attempting to present an equal-opportunities approach.

First, let me take suggestions made by Sue Watts (1987). She includes a useful list of general principles for science education which promotes equal opportunities. This was initially developed by

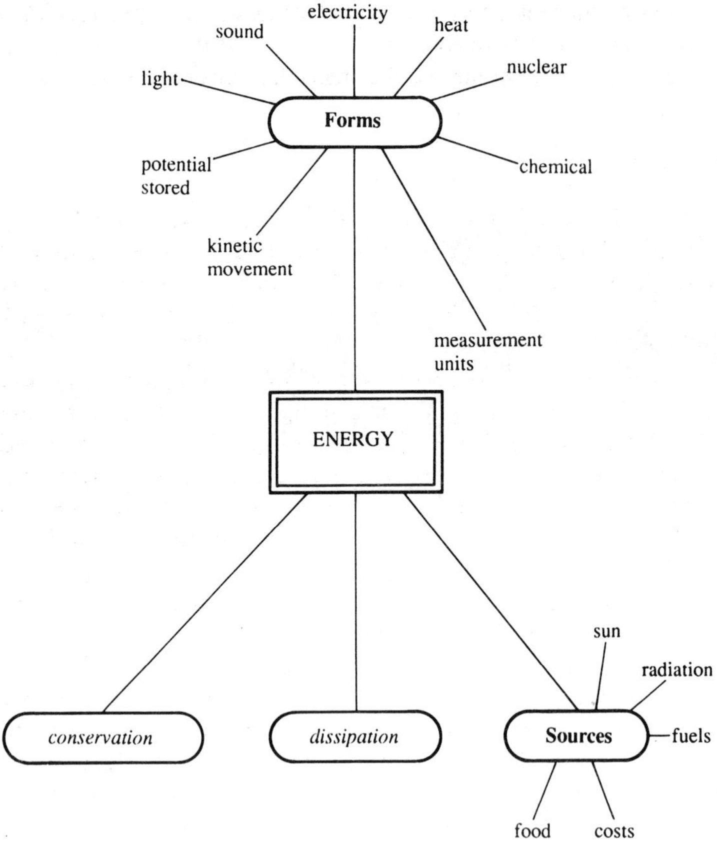

Figure 8.1

a group of science teachers and educators at a Commission for Racial Equality (CRE) workshop. Teachers should

- Incorporate a global perspective
- Understand issues relating to justice and equality
- Elaborate science in its social, political and economic context
- Make apparent the distribution of and access to power
- Make all people involved in science overt and not hidden
- Incorporate a historical perspective
- Start from and value the experience and knowledge of children

- Use flexible teaching and learning strategies and give emphasis to the learning of science
- Integrate practical approaches with the work as a whole

An example in practice

If I take a topic such as energy to be presented to key stage 3 pupils in Year 8, I would probably look initially at the programmes of study and then Attainment Target 13. Alternatively I could think about all the areas I might like to include. This might look something like Figure 8.1.

If I then decided to try to use the principles from the CRE group, particularly incorporating a global perspective, and starting from and valuing the experience and knowledge of children, I would probably arrive at a very different curriculum outline. Figure 8.2 shows one devised by a group of teachers which tries to take into account both these factors and thoughts about the published resources available in their departments, while at the same time using information about what the pupils had covered in previous topics in both secondary and primary school. In this outline the topic started with the familiar experiences and knowledge of pupils — Mars Bars and Readybrek, which both use advertisements about the amount of energy in the products. The pupils were encouraged to investigate the ingredients of the products, the origin of the ingredients, the use of energy in making the products and energy received from the products, and to make judgements about the efficiency of this use of energy. This meant that pupils were examining science in its social, economic and political context. After work on energy in other foods the topic then developed in two different directions: one directly related to food, and the other to fuels and fuel efficiency; both could lead into work on Chernobyl. These areas allowed pupils to cover the same knowledge and understanding as in the first diagram, but also covered many of the criteria outlined in the CRE list.

A process approach

Another approach to a topic could be to start with a question, preferably pupil-generated, and see what other possible questions

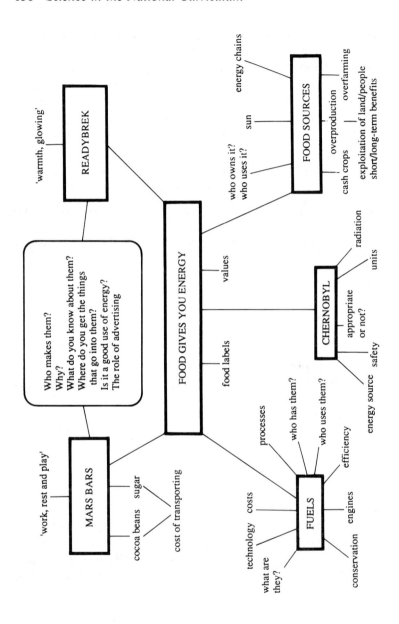

Figure 8.2

could come from this. In the second stage, decide what possible processes/skills could be easily drawn forth from the question, for example 'Why did the bicycle rust?' (see Figure 8.3).

This approach could ensure that OATs 1 and 17 become an integral part of the science curriculum, but the questions addressed (and therefore the direction of the curriculum) can be based on questions relevant to the pupil and present a 'real world' context.

Individual lessons

Another way in which the an equal-opportunities approach to the curriculum can be developed is in single lessons. An example of a specific lesson might be in trying to help pupils understand AT 10:6:3:

> understand that the effect of a turning force depends on where it is applied in relation to a pivot and its line of action.

The usual examples chosen for demonstrating this effect are a pulley, a hammer, a screwdriver and a brace. These examples might have a lot of relevance to a DIY enthusiast but have little relevance or interest to many 13-year-old pupils. Other, more appropriate examples could be used: kitchen tongs, a mixer, scissors, a pulley drawing water from a well. Some of these could, in fact, be brought into the classroom.

Such examples start from experiences known to the learner but then move into newer dimensions, including global ones (such as the method for raising water from a well). These examples are not just trying to be 'girl-friendly' or 'culture-friendly' but contextualize the science so that it is familiar and unthreatening, before presenting learners with more challenging situations. They also attempt to widen pupils' perception of what counts as science by suggesting that the everyday context is accessible to scientific interpretations, and that people throughout the world are involved in science or scientific pursuits. The context for science does not have to be 'high tech' and Western.

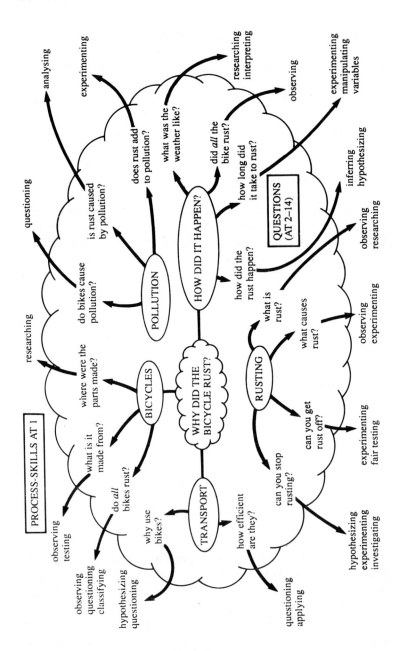

Figure 8.3 Why did the bicycle rust?

Changing the context

AT 4 could possibly be taught in a very clinical and theoretical way. Yet if it is integrated with AT 17 and presented as an 'issues-based' approach, much of the learning can be both relevant to pupils and make the people in science overt, showing the distribution of and access to power.

For instance, in my own teaching with a group of 13–14-year-old, mainly Bangladeshi, pupils I used their knowledge of genetic fingerprinting as a way of examining parts of AT 4. Current immigration practice for children trying to join their parent(s) in Britain from Bangladesh means that some are subjected to genetic fingerprinting techniques. Many of the pupils in my class knew this was being done and it therefore became the obvious stimulus to learning about genetics. However, it was not just left as an approach to genetics; we developed discussions on the use of science for these purposes as a whole-class project, and it was then taken up by both the drama and the English teachers as topic work for the class.

If I had the chance to repeat the topic, Figure 8.4 shows how I would develop it in the light of an equal-opportunities approach.

Using published materials

No teacher (no matter how dedicated) can possibly devise all his or her materials. Teaching is stressful enough without being given the extra burden. There are now some publications that can be used and adapted in order to develop equality of opportunity.

One example is parts of the *Science in Process* (ILEA/HEB, 1987) materials. In this, an equal-opportunities approach can start to be developed by integrating PC 2 with AT 1 (Exploration of Science) and AT 17 (The Nature of Science).

The activity 'World Energy Sources' from *Science in Process* (ILEA/HEB, 1987) starts from pupils' own experiences, moves them towards slightly familiar energy sources in the UK, then into the unfamiliar world of science, introducing ideas of the social, economic and political reasoning behind the use of energy resources.

In teaching AT 5 it is perhaps somewhat easier to see how to include a more global perspective but it is important that pupils can see how they can influence the direction of change. In the students'

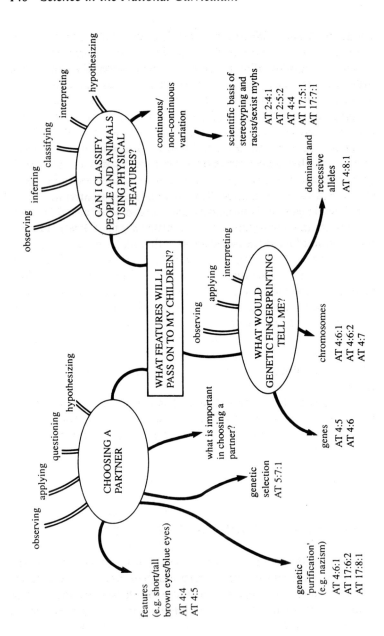

Figure 8.4 What features will I pass on to my children?

Guide, *In Science Kaleidoscope* (Hoyle *et al.*, 1990), the section on 'Recycling' (1:16) clearly outlines local and global issues related to recycling but also allows pupils the realization that science is influenced by social and economic factors: people's choices *can* affect the direction in which science is used.

Another example is SATIS (1986), materials which are already used by many teachers. They pertain to many aspects of PC 2 and introduce the social context and implications of science. However, in my view they sometimes stop short of dealing with the overtly economic and therefore political nature of many social decisions involved in the use of science. It is not always easy to deal with these, but to avoid politics is to neglect one of the important criteria for developing an equal-opportunities approach – making apparent the distribution of, and access to, power.

In *Science in Process* (ILEA/HEB, 1987) the activity 'Pesticides' (3.11) shows the historical context of DDT. The social implications are outlined by both the information on the page and the 'cut-out' activity provided in the teachers' materials, and pupils are encouraged to take the issue further in a role-play exercise. This approach encourages several of the aspects suggested in the CRE guidelines, including developing teaching and learning strategies, some of which are outlined in the non-statutory guidance (NCC, 1990) on AT 17.

Published materials can be useful in helping establish a firmer basis for an equal-opportunities approach but it will probably be a long time before they will automatically do the job for us. It is teachers' own awareness and understanding of the issues involved in justice and equality that remain the key to developing equality of opportunity.

TEACHING AND LEARNING APPROACHES

Besides considering their own awareness and understanding and the content of the materials and curriculum they use, the other major area in which teachers can ensure that pupils have equality of access to the curriculum is in the *teaching and learning strategies* employed in the classroom.

One of the CRE principles for establishing an equal-opportunities approach listed earlier was:

- use flexible teaching and learning strategies and give emphasis to the learning of science.

We need to develop flexible teaching and learning approaches which incorporate all the ideas listed in the non-statutory guidance in order to provide equality of opportunity.

Part A of the non-statutory guidance (NCC, 1990), paragraph 7.10, lists criteria from which teachers can select particular learning experiences for their pupils. These include giving the pupils opportunities to:

- develop attitudes appropriate to working scientifically
- work cooperatively and communicate scientific ideas to others
- develop an understanding of the relationship of scientific ideas to spiritual, ethical and moral dilemmas
- make use of materials that appeal to both boys and girls and those of all cultural backgrounds

All of these are highly commendable criteria and pertinent to equality of opportunity, but how are teachers supposed to ensure that they occur? The document also states that the National Curriculum 'demands the development of an increasing independence in pupils, and responsibility for their own learning'. It suggests that the teacher will be crucial in achieving this independence. It lists the following possible roles for the teacher: enabler, manager, presenter, adviser, observer, challenger, respondent, evaluator.

Building upon previous experience

One of the messages clearly emphasized in the last section is to give status to, and develop, pupils' own ideas. When doing this it is important to ensure that the ethos of the classroom supports pupils in developing their independence. This can be done in a variety of small and large ways. When acknowledging, using and building on pupils' ideas it is important to be sensitive to the contribution that their background may have made to their ideas. Without this teachers may discourage pupils from making further contributions; pupils may feel that their ideas are treated negatively.

There are different ways of accepting ideas, some of which may give stronger messages for equality than others. For example, at the beginning of a topic the teacher might start a class discussion by asking the pupils to 'put your hand up and tell me what ways you think there are of *communicating*'. The teacher goes on to take the ideas from a few in the class saying such things as

> 'Letters, um that's a good idea, Emma. Are there any really different ones. . . . Lee, what's your idea?'
> 'Oh you haven't got one.'
> 'Yes, now that's a really good one, Joseph, satellites are becoming very important nowadays. In science we use . . .'

It can be the tone of the teacher's reply, or the enthusiasm, that suggests to pupils that when they are asked for their ideas it is a matter of guessing what the teacher really wants to hear — the 'right-answer' mentality.

Many teachers have been aware of this kind of bias for a long time, so have tried a number of different approaches. One that really seems to value the pupils' ideas and uses them as a starting point for discussion could be as follows:

> 'Right now class. The new topic today is Communication. In threes or fours I want you to think of as many ways as you can of "communicating". Come up with one list for the group and then try to decide which ones you'd like to know more about. You've got 10 minutes then I want each group to present their ideas to the class. I'll be coming around if you've got anything you want to discuss. Away you go.'

This approach means the teacher can circulate around the class and listen carefully to what pupils are saying to see what they already know and what they are interested in, to build upon and develop the ideas. The teacher's role here is one of *observer and manager* (as suggested by the non-statutory guidance). Teachers also need to ensure that groups are working fairly and effectively so that no *one* person is being dominant and other pupils are not being isolated. It also means that *all* pupils have a chance to contribute to the discussion, not just those who put up their hands. Special-needs and bilingual pupils are also supported by this approach as they can contribute in their own way, and have their ideas counted, but in an informal, small group.

Teachers' role

This approach relies on creating an atmosphere in the classroom in which pupils are happy to contribute to discussions and listen to one another. Teachers know that it takes time for empathy and turn-taking skills to develop amongst pupils. But in an equal-opportunities approach it is essential to spend time developing these skills, so that pupils learn to value their own and other people's contributions. Only in this way will pupils feel more secure in discussing worries, such as incidents of racism, sexism or bullying.

Teachers have an important role in this. If pupils are to collaborate, and benefit from that collaboration by building upon one another's strengths, the teacher needs to organize the groups and monitor the collaboration taking place. For some tasks it will be appropriate to have mixed-gender, mixed-experience and mixed-ability groups, whereas for others it will be appropriate to have less mixed groups. The nature of the group will depend on the task. For example, if the task mainly requires skills of reading and writing (such as reporting an investigation) then some pupils need support. It may be best in this case to create mixed-language-competence groups so that pupils can build upon each other's skills in reading and writing while simultaneously developing their understanding of the science involved.

If the task is an experimental or problem-solving one it may be appropriate for some groups to be single sex, giving girls confidence to tackle tasks in their own way. The important point in both cases is that the teacher's role becomes one of *enabler* and *manager* rather than *presenter*.

The question of power relationships within the classroom is an important one in equal-opportunities work. Obviously the teacher has considerable power but the amount and the way he or she chooses to share it is important. As a *presenter, challenger, respondent* the teacher generally has a lot of control and could dominate what the pupils do and say. These roles (particularly that of presenter) mean that the pupils have very little control of what they can do and, as a result, may have very little control or responsibility for their learning. The role of *adviser* or *observer* means that the teacher is handing responsibility to the pupil. Initially, this can be very worrying for the teacher and quite disorientating for the pupil but it does enable pupils to begin to take more ownership of their learning. Again the manner in which teachers do this will give the pupils important clues to how they actually view the importance of this kind of teaching strategy.

Recognizing prejudice

Another important area is the active involvement of pupils in their science activities. In this case teachers act as *enablers, advisers* and *observers*. To develop an equal-opportunities approach requires making sure that pupils develop a variety of roles in the classroom. We are all well aware of the documented stereotyped roles that pupils can undertake in a classroom (or teachers think they undertake) – boys doing the technical things while girls make the written work look nice. Pupils need to develop a whole range of different strategies and teachers need to monitor who does what in order to ensure that they are providing a range of learning experiences to which pupils can respond. Teachers also need to be aware of their own prejudice. How often have you heard 'that Samantha is a right little madam, just like her sister', or 'I think it's the whole family. Just look at that brother and those cousins. Mind you, what can you expect coming from . . .'?

We all harbour prejudice that can be negative but we also have 'feelings' about pupils, many of which are part of the basis of our professional judgements. What we need to recognize is the difference between 'feelings' based on reliable and valid evidence and 'feelings' resulting from prejudices that are invalid and negative. For an equal-opportunities approach it is important that *all* our professional judgements are based on valid and reliable evidence.

Positive approaches

There are other activities that teachers can ensure are carried out in the classroom to ensure equality of opportunities. For example, pupils' work can be displayed well in the room and corridors, which gives pupils the message that their contribution counts. Any other display work, such as commercial posters, should have a balance of women, men, black and white people and present global situations, including the social implications of science, if pupils are to experience a balanced view of science and to absorb the implications of OAT 17. Resources such as books, standard technical materials (glassware, Bunsen burners and so on) and stationery can be labelled and easily accessible to pupils so that they get the message that the learning environment is pleasant and responsive to their needs if they respect it. Obviously this means the removal of any offensive or derogatory graffiti. In a similar vein it is important that teachers challenge incidents of inequality—such as bullying, name calling, stereotyping, graffiti on books—and not just let incidents go, thinking that 'kids are cruel' or 'if you make a fuss, then it will get out of all proportion'.

If teachers ignore obvious incidents it conveys the message that the teacher doesn't really care. As a result pupils may become less likely to respond when teachers offer them more responsibility for their learning, and they will view school as a place of injustice.

DIFFERENTIATION

The way in which differentiation is tackled within the science curriculum can be of vital importance to an equal-opportunities approach. Ways in which pupils can be offered a differentiated approach to the curriculum include (a) providing materials at different levels on the same topic; (b) giving pupils the same task but letting them produce different outcomes; or (c) grouping pupils in mixed-experience/ability groups so that they can bring and take different things from a task. All these are valuable approaches depending on the task, situation and the learner. In a classroom where an equal-opportunities approach is operating, pupils should be exposed to a range of possible strategies; they should not always be working on the same materials and being judged by their outcome. Nor should they only be given materials at the 'level they seem to work best at' as this can undervalue any development or creativity they may be able to show. Dividing pupils into different groupings can often be used as a way of giving them a differentiated approach. They bring different skills to a task, and group work can help pupils build upon their own and others' competence and thus help them to different levels of understanding. The suggestions on differentiation offered in the science non-statutory guidance concentrate on giving pupils different materials or situations to which to respond. They need to be expanded for an equal-opportunities approach.

Special-needs or bilingual pupils are often the impetus for teachers to consider differentiation. *All* pupils need language development as part of their schooling, and research shows that this is best done in and through each subject area. An equal-opportunities approach to science education would want to ensure that science lessons are an easy situation in which to develop pupils' language skills and in particular the skills of bilingual and special educational needs (SEN) pupils. A range of approaches is needed in materials, teaching methods and the ethos of the classroom.

Special educational needs

The National Curriculum emphasizes the need for all pupils to have access to science learning. The NCC document *Curriculum for All* (NCC, 1989b) outlines an approach to science for pupils with special educational needs. Many of the ideas mentioned have already been considered in this chapter:

- It is open-ended and allows for the same task to be developed to different levels of achievement.
- It recognizes pupils' own contributions and experiences and builds on them.
- It starts at the level of competence of the pupil and consequently encourages greater self-confidence.
- It encourages group work and group skills.
- The teacher can switch activities and tasks according to the pervading working atmosphere.
- It can be used with different age groups depending on the materials selected and interests of the pupils.
- It builds on previous experience and gives pupils with special educational needs the confidence to tackle new areas.

These points are not new to most SEN departments or science teachers, but actually attempting to carry them out with pupils with severe learning difficulties may seem daunting.

Figure 8.5 shows an example of the science part of a school topic plan that one severe learning difficulties school undertook in the spring term of 1990. It shows that although the pupils were in

CLASS 6	CLASS 7	CLASS 8	BEECHWOOD
(1) Colour, shape and texture Size of clothes/material AT 1:1:1 – observing familiar ... 1:2:2 – identify simple differences ... 1:2:4 – list and collate observations ... 6:1:1 – describe familiar and unfamiliar objects in terms of properties ... 9:2:4 – sort materials into broad groups ...	(1) Clothes for different activities – special clothes for special situations – which material is best for keeping out rain? Making an umbrella? Waterproofing? – clothes for keeping warm or cool, what kind of cloth is best for keeping warm? AT 1:1:1 – observe ... 6:1:1 1:2:1 – ask questions ... 6:1:2 1:2:2 – identify differences ... 1:3:1 – formulate hypotheses ...	(1) Distinguishing between different fabrics – naming and identifying fabrics (e.g. cotton, linen, silk, nylon) – classifying as natural or 'man-made'. (2) Observing different fabrics – looking at fabrics under a hand lens and noting differences AT 6:1:1 6:2:2 6:3:1 6:3:2	(1) Keeping clean – ways of keeping the body clean (2) Cleaning and caring for clothes – examining washing powders – examining soaps and detergents – the effects of washing on fabrics, of washing machines and irons. AT 1:3:3 1:3:6 1:3:7 1:4:1 1:4:2 6:2:1 6:4:1 6:4:2

(2) Seasonal clothing, wearing different
clothes in different seasons
 	
AT
9:1:1 – know variety of weather
conditions ...
9:2:1 – weather has a powerful effect on
people's lives ...
16:1:1 – describe seasonal changes ...
1:7:2 – curiosity ...
	Attitudes AT 6:1:1
	Curiosity 6:1:2
	Participation 6:3:2
	             9:1:1
	             9:1:2
		(3) Qualities of fabrics
		– insulation effects
		– strength
		
		AT
		6:4:1
		6:4:2
		10:3:1
		10:4:1
			(3) Dyes and dyeing
			– the effects of colour and light
			– dyeing natural and synthetic
			fabrics
			– different types of dye
			– indicators from plants
			– chromatography
			
			AT
			15:1:1
			15:1:2
			15:2:2
			8:4:1
			7:4:1
			7:4:2

(3) Types of different fabrics – distinguishing between cotton, wool, nylon AT 9:2:4 – sort materials into broad groups ...	(2) Fabrics around the house – identifying names of materials – purposes for fabrics used in the home (colour, texture, insulation, comfort, etc.) – testing materials' (e.g. floor coverings) wear and tear – use of materials (e.g. plastics, metals) – sound insulation AT 1:1:1 – observe ... 1:2:1 – ask questions ... 1:2:2 – identify differences ... 1:3:1 – formulate hypotheses ... Attitudes Curiosity Criticism of results Cooperation	(4) Who needs special clothing? – relating clothing to special purposes (e.g. firefighting, police, sport) – camouflage of animals AT 1:3:1 2:3:3 15:1:2 (5) Symmetry – looking at symmetry in clothing (e.g. gloves, socks) (6) Making cloth – weaving fabrics – paper making – tie dyeing	(4) Weaving – making cloth – making paper AT 7:4:2 7:5:1

Figure 8.5 Woodlands—clothes topic—science outline

different classes, though not necessarily of different ages, the same topic could be developed at different levels so as to build upon pupils' previous experience. The plan was successfully used in classes 8 and 9. In class 10 the plan was too ambitious, but through this experience the teachers felt that pupils could build confidence by repeating aspects of clothing in the next topic (holidays and transport).

Many teachers dealing with pupils with severe learning difficulties are currently considering working towards/within level 1, whereas teachers dealing with pupils with moderate learning difficulties are attempting to look carefully at the levels which their pupils can attempt (levels 1–3/4) and deciding how the programme of study and each statement of attainment can be broken down into more manageable parts so as not to overwhelm both teachers and pupils.

Pupils with special educational needs in mainstream schools are dealt with by *Science in the National Curriculum* (DES, 1989). Most of the suggestions it makes are the same as those in the section on differentiation, but it is important to add that catering for these pupils is essential to any equal-opportunities approach.

Assessment

The National Curriculum introduces to schools not only a set agenda of what to teach but a whole, as yet undefined, system of teacher and national assessment. The aims of assessment as defined by the National Curriculum include increasing motivation of pupils as well as having a system whereby parents and other consumers can ascertain how well pupils are doing. There is a distinct problem with the motivation argument, particularly as regards equal opportunities. Pupils for whom schooling is a positive experience will get a lot of satisfaction from the information they receive from both teacher assessments and standard assessment tasks (SATs). Yet for a large proportion of students, particularly black students and girls, science education is not a positive experience. The information they are likely to receive from the assessment will only confirm their ability to fail – not very motivating.

If teachers use assessment to plan the next steps for pupils to take or constantly to monitor and adapt the curriculum and the experiences they are offering to pupils, then there might be some benefits from the system. But this is a big 'might' and it requires that the assessment methods used are appropriate. Studies in social psychology have shown us that most tests are class and culturally biased. We have no reason to suppose that despite all efforts the SATs tests of the National Curriculum will not suffer from this bias, especially considering that most of the people writing them are white and middle-class. Similarly, teacher assessments are likely to suffer in this way. Teachers are being encouraged to adopt different methods of assessment: systematic observations, discussions with pupils, marking pupils' work, as well as the standard end-of-unit tests and GCSE-type practical tests. Ostensibly teachers are supposed to find out what pupils know and can do. Presumably any low expectations or stereotyped notions teachers have of pupils will be reflected in their attempts at assessment. Teachers will of course be offered moderation, but will it be a panacea for all their worries? I doubt it. We will have to wait and see how the assessment element of the National Curriculum turns out.

All that has been said about developing equal opportunities in this chapter relies in many ways upon cogs in the system — teachers raising their awareness of both the issues and how to employ strategies to change their approaches and instigate new ones. This will require action from individual teachers, schools, LEAs, universities, teacher-training institutions, assessment teams and professional bodies. The Association for Science Education has produced policy documents on gender and multicultural education and associated INSET materials which may be helpful in getting teachers to consider what they can do (see, for example ASE, 1990). Hopefully the NCC will also provide support and materials in order to make sure that equality of opportunities is a reality, not just a nice heading in the documentation.

REFERENCES

ASE [Association of Science Education] (1990) Science and multicultural education. *Education and Science*, January 1990, pp. 67–85. A document discussing science and multicultural education and an introduction to the ASE Multicultural Working Party.

Bentley, D. and Watts, D. M. (1986). Courting the positive virtues: a case for feminist science. *European Journal of Science Education*, **8**, 121–34.

DES [Department of Education and Science] and the Welsh Office (1989)

Science in the National Curriculum: Statutory and Non-Statutory Guidance. London: HMSO.

Hoyle, P., Laine, C. and Smyth, P. (1990) Recycling. In *Science Kaleidoscope: A Student's Guide to Key Stage 3*. London: Heinemann Educational Books.

Hussey, M. (1982) Education in a multiethnic society. *Multiethnic Education Review*, 1(2), 6–7.

ILEA/HEB (1987) *Science in Process*. London: Inner London Education Authority/Heinemann Educational Books.

NCC [National Curriculum Council] (1989a) *The National Curriculum and Whole Curriculum Planning: Preliminary Guidance*. Circular No. 6. York: National Curriculum Council.

NCC [National Curriculum Council] (1989b) *Curriculum for All: Special Needs in the National Curriculum*. Circular No. 2. York: National Curriculum Council.

NCC [National Curriculum Council] (1990) *Science: Non-Statutory Guidance*. York: National Curriculum Council.

Russell, T. and Munby, H. (1989) Science as a discipline. Science as seen by students and teachers' professional knowledge. In Millar, R. (ed.) *Doing Science: Images of Science in Science Education*. The Falmer Press, pp. 107–25.

SATIS [Science and Technology in Society] (1986) Hatfield: Association for Science Education.

Watts, S. (1987). Approaches to curriculum development from both an anti-racist and a multicultural perspective. In *Better Science: Working for a Multicultural Society*. London: Secondary Science Curriculum Review/Heinemann Educational Books, p. 19.

Chapter 9

Key Stage 5: Science and Post-16 Education

Dick West and Cathy Wilson

We start and finish this chapter with quotations drawn from the same source which typify two contrasting approaches to teaching and learning. The first refers to a narrowly specialized programme taught, in large part, in a depersonalized manner. The concluding quotation illustrates a more open and student-centred approach that is no less challenging and intellectually demanding.

> When he was still a small boy his father left their country home to start a laundry in Manchester; Chadwick's grandmother seems to have raised him. He sat for two scholarships to the University of Manchester at sixteen, an early age even in the English educational system, won them both, kept one and went off to the university. He meant to read mathematics. The entrance interviews were held publicly in a large, crowded hall. Chadwick got into the wrong line. He had already begun to answer the lecturer's questions when he realised he was being questioned for a physics course. Since he was too timid to explain, he decided that the physics lecturer impressed him and he would read for physics. The first year he was sorry, his biographers report, 'the physics classes were large and noisy.' The second year he heard Rutherford lecture on his early New Zealand experiments and was converted.
>
> (Rhodes, 1986)

In this chapter we set out to review some of the significant attempts that are being made to change the nature of post-16 science education and the post-16 curriculum in general. After considering the pressures for change and presenting brief accounts of recent developments, we conclude with a discussion of the sort of radical reforms needed in the whole system of post-16 provision in England

and Wales if access is to be widened and participation rates increased.

CURRENT PROVISION

Current educational provision in England and Wales for 16–19-year-olds in schools, colleges, and colleges of further education consists of either a wide range of vocational and pre-vocational programmes accredited by a diverse cluster of agencies, or the study of a limited range of academic subjects at AS or A level examined by a variety of different examination boards. The system also makes provision for some students to retake GCSE examinations in the hope of improving their grades. What the system as a whole currently lacks is coherence and it provides little by way of logical continuity and progression from the National Curriculum implemented in 1989. It is important to note that there is growing criticism of vocational, pre-vocational and academic education. Vocational education is attacked for being too specific in terms of skill development and for lacking a broad academic context, whereas academic education is criticized on the grounds that it is too specialized and that in one sense it is *narrowly* vocational. A further, and powerful, criticism of current provision is that it is inherently elitist, and this manifests itself in the participation rate, or rather non-participation rate, in post-16 education and training. Almost 60 per cent of young people in the age cohort do not participate in it and only 12 per cent of those who do continue into higher education. Participation may be limited by local factors such as size of sixth forms and ease of access to colleges of further education, but of far greater concern is an apparent discrimination which is reflected in terms of under-representation of certain social classes, ethnic groups and within certain geographical regions.

Another key feature of current provision is the high failure rate built into the system. Smithers and Robinson (1989) point out in *Increasing Participation in Higher Education* that over 40 per cent of young people have failed GCE O level and of those who went on to take A level a further 30 per cent failed:

> In 1987, only about 14 per cent of school leavers obtained two A levels, the basic requirement for going on to higher education, and nearly half (47.6%) obtained no qualifications to speak of.

Moreover, the 14 per cent obtaining two A levels included all grades down to E.

PRESSURES FOR CHANGE

Various attempts have been made to rationalize provision and to increase the participation rate and there are currently many pressures, from industry, the professional institutes, higher education and government, to bring about reform. Those with long memories will recall the Q and F, and N and F debates in the mid-1970s, and some may remember the ill-fated Certificate of Extended Education (CEE). More recently there has been a spate of influential papers advocating change. These include *The Path to Higher Education: An Action Report* (Foundation for Science and Technology, 1987); 'The way forward: an alternative route for post-16 science studies' (ILEA/ASE/SSCR *ad hoc* group, 1988); *The 16-19 Science Curriculum and Its Assessment: A Statement of Policy* (Royal Society, 1988); the Higginson Report *Advancing A-levels* (HMSO, 1988); *16-19 Education and Training: A Statement* (Engineering Council and the Society of Education Officers, 1988); *Post-16 Science Studies: The A and AS-level Dimension* (ASE for ASE/CNAA/SCUE, 1989); *Planning 16-19 Education* (Secondary Heads Association, 1989); *Towards a Skills Revolution* (CBI, 1989); *Aim Higher: Widening Access to Higher Education* (Royal Society of Arts, 1989) and *Report of the 16-19 Physics Course Working Party* (Institute of Physics, 1990). The report by Sir Christopher Ball, *More Means Different: Widening Access to Higher Education* (Royal Society of Arts, May 1990), and the proposal to establish vocational A levels made by Sir John Cassels, *Britain's Real Skill Shortage* (Policy Studies Institute, May 1990), add further fuel to the fire. In spite of the rejection by government of the proposals in Chapter 3 of the Higginson Report, there are strong indications that major changes will take place over the next few years. For instance, the recent National Curriculum Council (NCC) response to the Secretary of State on the issue of core skills (NCC, 1990) is clearly relevant to other sections of the Higginson Report. Sir Roy Harding, a member of the Higginson Committee, argued persuasively at a recent seminar (Hatfield Polytechnic, 22 November 1989) that most of the proposals in the report apart from the concept of five leaner and tougher A levels were being implemented, or would be in the very near future.

CONTINUITY AND PROGRESSION

The introduction of the National Curriculum with science as a core subject for all pupils aged 5 to 16 will in itself lead to changes in post-16 provision. The government has asked the NCC and the Schools Examination and Assessment Council (SEAC) to consider issues of continuity and progression in post-16 provision from the baseline of Attainment Targets and programmes of study at key stage 4. In addition, and following Kenneth Baker's speech to the Association of Colleges of Further and Higher Education (ACFHE) in February 1989, the NCC and SEAC have been asked to consider which core skills should be incorporated in the programmes of work of 16–19-year-olds following AS- and A-level studies and what the implication would be for other students in the age group. Finally, the Secretary of State has asked SEAC to work towards a rationalization of, and reduction in, the number of AS- and A-level syllabuses on offer, and to develop general principles to govern these examinations. It is significant that, at this stage in educational development, an examination introduced as long ago as 1951 does not appear to have any general principles embedded in it. Perhaps the problem is that the principles that epitomize A level are no longer considered valid and relevant.

If, or when, changes are introduced as a result of these pressures, they are likely to cause problems for teachers similar to those they now face as a result of the introduction of the National Curriculum. First, there is the problem of building a post-16 curriculum from a set of subject-based imperatives that govern the curriculum 5–16 and not from a rationale for the curriculum as a whole. We already know that the lack of a rationale for the National Curriculum is creating many problems for schools and there is now clear evidence that senior politicians are worried by aspects of its implementation. There were even reports that Margaret Thatcher, when Prime Minister, said that 'the National Curriculum had not come out at all as she had intended—was much too detailed and prescriptive, and it took up too much teaching time, detracting from teachers' own judgment and creativity' (*Education*, 1990).

It is also likely to be difficult to achieve a match in continuity and progression from key stage 4 to AS- and A-level syllabuses which were not designed as an extension to the content and processes incorporated in the National Curriculum. Similar problems exist in matching a subject-based National Curriculum to programmes such as BTEC which are based on the development of core skills and competencies.

Secondly, recent ministerial statements on incorporating core skills in 16–19 programmes present several problems in terms of modernizing existing syllabuses and approaches to course design and assessment. It is always difficult to graft 'new ideas' on to dated systems and structures, especially in education. We all know that one major cause of the failure of comprehensive secondary education in Britain was the attempt to graft the concept of education for all to the notion of a grammar school curriculum. It is clear from the response on core skills published by the NCC (1990) that there is a widespread acceptance of the six core skills proposed by Mr Baker. In his speech to ACFHE, the then Secretary of State for Education and Science defined a skill as 'a competence based on knowledge and understanding' and listed the core skills as: communication — written or oral; numeracy; personal relations; familiarity with technology; familiarity with systems; and familiarity with changing working and social systems. The new Secretary of State then asked the NCC and SEAC to consider how these skills could be incorporated in AS- and A-level examinations and more broadly within the post-16 curriculum. In its response the NCC has broadly endorsed the six skills (or skill clusters) and the 16–19 Task Group has recommended the inclusion of the following in the study programme of *all* 16–19-year-olds:

1. communication
2. problem solving
3. personal skills
4. numeracy
5. information technology
6. modern language competence

It is expected that these same skills will be endorsed by SEAC. The NCC has recommended that the first three should be embedded, and wherever possible be an aspect of syllabus design, in all AS- and A-level syllabuses. The remaining three skills should be incorporated into total curricular provision for all students. It also proposes that the skills embedded in AS- and A-level syllabuses should be assessed as clearly defined Attainment Targets, should influence the grades awarded and should be reported in records of achievement. The other three core skills would be reported only in records of achievement. These records will include references to AS- and A-level subjects, additional studies, cross-curricular themes, work experience and projects.

The NCC had previously identified five cross-curricular themes for the 5-16 curriculum:

economic and industrial understanding
environmental education
education for citizenship
careers education and guidance
health education

It now proposes that the post-16 curriculum should include these five themes, plus two more:

scientific and technological understanding
aesthetic and creative understanding

in order to create an element of broadening at this level. In short it is proposing the development of scientific and technological understanding as a core element in all post-16 programmes of study. Finally, the NCC proposes that work experience should be carefully planned and structured and used to develop core skills. 'It should be part of a student's entitlement' (NCC, 1990).

While welcoming much of the above we do see significant problems, as already indicated, in incorporating much of this in academic subject syllabuses at AS and A level, given that the delivery of such core skills is not an explicit component of the National Curriculum and there are few specific skill attainment targets stated within it. It is also difficult to see the development of major cross-curricular themes for students who are determined to follow a narrowly specialized three-A-level programme in, say, physics and double mathematics or physics, chemistry and biology. We appear to be heading for many of the same problems at post-16 as we have over matching key stage 4 of the National Curriculum to GCSE. These problems are inherent in any curricular reform that is done piecemeal.

Thirdly, we foresee major problems in the exercise of rationalizing and generating basic principles at this stage for AS- and A-level examinations which were designed, or derived from, a system developed in the 1950s to serve the needs of selective secondary education and an explicit policy of minority access to post-16 and higher education. It appears that the government is attempting to fit a modernization of curricular provision to a system of assessment and examining without altering the system at all. Or is it? There is clear evidence that the Education Secretary is considering not only an intermediate qualification between GCSE and A levels (remember CEE?), but also the possibility of modular programmes and the key issue of credit transfer between vocational and academic courses. It can be argued that any attempt to bolt on to existing curricular provision major changes such as core skills and cross-curricular themes without undertaking a fundamental review of the purpose and nature of post-16 education and training will create major implementation problems for schools, colleges, employers and higher education.

NEW DEVELOPMENTS IN POST-16 EDUCATION

Having looked at likely changes to provision we are now in a position to review some of the new developments that are being introduced in post-16 science education and which address some of the problems alluded to above. Our first examples utilize the concept of A-level enhancement in delivering a broader range of skills, including what are likely to be designated as the core skills.

The Yorkshire, Humberside and North-East Enhancement Project started with five northern LEAs that were looking at the implications of TVEI entitlement post-16, especially for A-level students. The project is seeking to develop programmes that build on pre-16 provision within an 'entitlement' framework related to the knowledge, skills and understanding that students will need in terms of their future personal and career development. These programmes are designed to meet individual needs and therefore rely on a process of negotiation, guidance and counselling. Programmes are structured within a Certificate of Pre-Vocational Education framework and, while concentrating on A levels (fourteen A-level subjects are currently being considered), may also lead to BTEC qualifications.

The three main thrusts of the project are centred on *student*, *subject* and *support*, with an individual student's programme including a 'core' defined in terms of skills and understanding, and 'enrichments' including work experience, residential experience, cross-curricular applications of technology and records of achievement.

The SATIS 16–19 Project (ASE, 1990) also aims to enhance post-16 science provision through a wide range of resources providing support for both general education and the enrichment of specialist academic and vocational science courses. SATIS units are designed to meet the growing demand for science teaching programmes which seek to foster the qualities of mind that are needed in a changing world, including the ability to think, to act, to apply as well as receive knowledge and to communicate effectively. A particular feature of SATIS 16–19 materials is the utilization of a very comprehensive range of teaching and learning approaches, which we will illustrate later in this chapter.

A second approach is through the concept of A-level programme enrichment where the post-16 programme is extended by means of an additional study element. The North-West/University of Liverpool TVEI scheme is one example of this. It is based on group project work of increasing complexity and is open to all students irrespective of the number and nature of A levels studied. Three required projects, of increasing complexity, are designed to encourage the development of skills and processes relevant to the world of work. These have been identified by schools, industry and higher education working in collaboration. They include setting targets, working to deadlines, developing the interactive skills needed for group work, decision making, organizational skills, information handling and communication. The subject and nature of the final project involves active negotiation with local industry, business, commerce and/or an institution of higher education. Assessment is undertaken on a group basis and is validated by the University of Liverpool, which provides a record of achievement.

Similarly, the joint Staffordshire and Walsall Post-16 Project aims to promote team work between students and industrialists through the generation and execution of problem-solving exercises. These are specifically related to science and technology but are designed to be used in general studies and with interdisciplinary groups. The project is producing a guide for teachers and students and a wide range of courseware/software, including action notes, that incorporate problems which cannot be investigated in a short time. A particular aim of the project is to enable students to simulate long-term environmental problems.

Thirdly, there are approaches such as the Wessex, Cambridge and the North-West TVEI modular scheme which seek to provide for greater student choice of study programmes, enhanced student motivation as a result of shorter-term learning objectives and, possibly, the benefits of improved staff/student ratios.

The Wessex Project involves schools and further education colleges in the development of modular courses which contain a compulsory core of A-level subject material that is taught in traditional style and assessed by standard external examinations. However, various models for transacting the core in different subject areas have been developed and in some cases the examination is taken at the end of the first year. The core represents 60 per cent of the course and the remaining 40 per cent consists of four complementary modules, selected from a module bank, which aim to provide breadth of study in both content and process. The modules are either issue based or thematic and, in science, foster the appreciation of science in the context of the real world, emphasize student-centred and active learning and encourage the development of a range of skills including study skills. A feature of the scheme is that complementary modules need not be drawn from the same subject bank as the core. For example, core biology can be supplemented by modules in geography or mathematics. The pilot scheme currently incorporates programmes in biology, chemistry, physics, design and technology, modern languages, business studies, art and design and economics. Mathematics, English and creative arts are also being developed. The scheme is currently limited to A level but it is hoped to extend it to include AS in due course, and in one further-education college an attempt is being made to establish a common first-year course, leading to BTEC or A level in Year 2.

The Cambridge Modular A level Science Project will operate under the University of Cambridge Local Examinations Syndicate (UCLES) module bank system and will enable students to gain a range of single-subject or double-award AS and A levels in biology, chemistry, physics or science. The scheme incorporates foundation modules in biology, chemistry and physics, optional subject-focused modules and extended-study modules. The modules, which are assessed and certificated on their completion, represent 40 hours of study time. AS awards are made on the basis of studying three modules, a single A level requires the study of six modules, and a double award, twelve modules. All awards require the appropriate foundation module(s) and an extended study module. The single and double award science require the study of all three foundation modules. The scheme aims to provide the opportunity for all students to study some of the broader aspects of science and to develop skills common to all scientific disciplines.

Finally, a group of LEAs in north-west England is developing a modular A-level science programme which aims to ensure continuity and progression from pre-16 modular schemes introduced as part of TVEI entitlement. Within a framework of scientific and cross-curricular transferable skills, students will be offered a range of modules that establish a foundation or set of foundation experiences. Additional modules at a variety of levels will build on these and lead to AS, A level or BTEC qualifications. Figure 9.1 indicates the model for development.

At present all these schemes are operating on a pilot basis and are restricted by SEAC to a limited number of approved centres and small numbers of candidates. These developments represent serious attempts to improve flexibility and introduce a greater diversity of teaching and learning approaches. The enhancement and modular schemes, while aiming to extend the boundaries of A level, are clearly constrained by the present framework and are to a greater or lesser extent based on existing syllabuses. As such, with the exception of the Wessex and North-West modular schemes, they do little to address other key issues in 16–19 provision, such as improving access and participation, and providing a bridge across the academic and vocational divide.

ENTITLEMENT FOR ALL POST-16

In order to address the issue of access and participation we feel it is important at this point to consider the question of entitlement and to explore some of the characteristics of an entitlement curriculum. An entitlement curriculum would be designed from the outset to be accessible to all post-16 students through various combinations of full-time and part-time study, private study and study in the workplace. Such a curriculum must be open as well as accessible and it

COMMON CORE OF MODULES
Providing a set of broad experiences

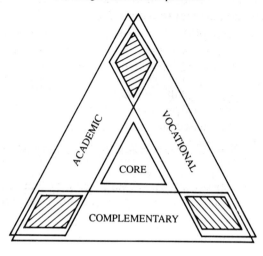

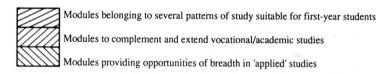

Modules belonging to several patterns of study suitable for first-year students

Modules to complement and extend vocational/academic studies

Modules providing opportunities of breadth in 'applied' studies

Figure 9.1 Model for development

must also be enabling. It must aim to improve educational and training opportunities and it must be relevant to the needs and aspirations of all individuals and groups of young people.

To be truly *open* the curriculum must:

provide for all students irrespective of their ability, aptitude, and career aspirations or intentions;

be fair and unbiased in terms of gender, age, ethnic, cultural, religious and socio-economic background of the student;

be encouraging and enabling with regard to students with handicap.

To be *accessible* the curriculum must:

be provided through a range of institutions so that access is not limited by the nature of employment, geographical location or simple demographic and economic factors;

be available through the full range of study patterns including full-time study, part-time study, private study, distance learning and supported self-study and study in the workplace;

be seen to be relevant to the perceived needs of students as well as to their actual needs.

To be *enabling* the curriculum must:

build on, and extend, the previous knowledge and skills gained by students;

provide a framework of studies and activities that encourages students to use new knowledge and skills in a purposeful and creative way;

help young people to succeed and not fail.

The curriculum must also deal centrally with:

the acquisition and utilization of knowledge and understanding — to know, understand and to be able to use knowledge;

the acquisition, understanding and utilization of skills — to know and develop skills, and be able to understand and use them;

the development of positive attitudes and values — to know and understand oneself, be self-aware, self-confident and aware of others;

the ability to deploy knowledge, skills and attitudes in a way that is appropriate to a range of general and specific contexts — to be competent and develop capability.

The traditional academic provision in 16–19 education has been largely content led and it can be argued that vocational training has been largely context led. An entitlement curriculum should be skill and competency led. It is only by meeting the above criteria that we will be able to create a post-16 curriculum that extends educational opportunities to all. Failure to achieve on any of the above parameters immediately restricts or caps equality of opportunity. When analysed against these criteria most aspects of current 16–19 academic and vocational provision are found wanting, which may go a long way towards explaining the very low participation rates that have traditionally been found in post-16 education and training in the UK.

In a recent paper on a structure for post-16 education, Bausor and Zachary point out that a major problem in defining an entitlement curriculum is

> the conflict between the desirable aims of *entitlement* and *diversity*. One of the reasons for the introduction of a National Curriculum was the failure of the option system used in most secondary schools to deliver an appropriate, coherent and agreed programme of education for all pupils; in emphasising *diversity* it neglected *entitlement*. On the other hand there is a real danger that in defining the *entitlement* of all students very precisely, and ensuring that it is met, one may fail to meet the great *diversity* of needs of different people.
>
> (Bausor and Zachary, 1990)

Drawing in part on an other paper, produced by members of the *ad hoc* ILEA/ASE/SSCR group — 'A question of entitlement: a contribution to the post-16 debate' (West, Zachary *et al.* (1990)) — we will now explore some of the characteristics of entitlement curriculum in science and consider how the tensions stated earlier might be avoided. An approach to an entitlement programme in science studies, as in other subject areas, would seek to incorporate three key elements in programme design. The first concerns the need for *preparation* — opening doors, keeping doors open, enabling students to make informed decisions and to acquire broadly based skills. The second element is *training* (which we use in a broader sense than narrow, skill-based training) whether it be academic, vocational, pre-vocational or combinations of the three. Finally the programme should contain an element that is to do with the *development* of the whole person.

Preparation could include:

careers counselling
communication skills
management skills
study skills including supported self-study
work experience

Training could include:

AS- and A-level work
academic work primarily below A-level standard

BTEC 1st Certificate
BTEC National Certificate
European baccalaureate
International baccalaureate

Development could include:

counselling
cross-curricular studies
dealing with change
education for leisure
philosophy
politics
religious education

While there may be elements of overlap between activities derived from the three facets of need, it is important to note that curricular provision which overemphasizes the training dimension is likely to inhibit access and the broadening of curricular provision which so many agencies are keen to see developed. A strong case can be made for an approach to curricular planning that fully integrates the preparation and development dimensions through significant changes to academic, vocational and pre-vocational syllabuses and courses.

Course structures must be flexible to cater for the varying needs of students. The three facets might be delivered through distinct modules or might be more fully integrated: for example, all academic work might have objectives that include clearly defined study skills. It is clear that the Secretary of State envisages a range of core skills, promoted through a common requirement across all syllabuses, as well as those which are subject specific. While supporting this in principle we also see it as critically important to address the developmental dimension of provision.

It seems likely that a modular approach to the curriculum would work best as far as the training facet is concerned. Initially every module could be clearly labelled, for example, 'A level' or 'BTEC National' or a foundation module for either. If, however, we are to move towards effective access, bridging and credit transfer arrangements between courses, future labels might specify level solely in terms of National Vocational Qualifications stages. Similarly the A-level boards might specify combinations of modules which would constitute a specific title, but again at a future date, and following the review of AS and A level required by the Secretary of State, the requirements of the A-level common cores might be modified to allow combinations of modules to become more student centred and better matched to career aspirations and experience gained through work placements.

The weighting of the different facets will need discussion, and certain aspects might be left open to negotiation with individual students. It will be very important not to let the training dimension assume too great a degree of dominance, as it does with the present AS- and A-level regime, or to prescribe too strictly the content and combinations of modules within it. Over-dominance, as indicated earlier, would militate against meeting the broader needs of the age group. Too tight a specification of modules, whether in terms of knowledge or highly task-specific skills, would restore the academic/vocational divide we are seeking to bridge. Either would destroy any continuity and progression from the pre-16 curriculum. It is important to note that recent thinking on the part of employers and universities has moved away from rigidity and inflexibility in content for entrance requirements. The CBI points out that

> As employers increasingly require the skills for adaptability and innovation in employment, education and training need to be broadly based, concerned not just with technical understanding of the job but competence in the broader work context. . . . Task competence is not enough to meet this need.
>
> (CBI, 1989)

Furthermore the work of the Open University has demonstrated that appropriate prior learning and experience are as relevant as formal academic qualifications for entry to undergraduate work.

In the longer term we would seek a BTEC approach to course design and accreditation at the local level. Schools and colleges would design courses, not teach to syllabuses, and would start from a framework of core skills and competencies. In the case of science courses they would use appropriate scientific subject matter to foster and develop these skills and competencies. In addition other subject contexts would be utilized to develop science skills and understanding: for example in history, the study of aspects of the history of science; in English, the critical reading of science fiction; and in religious education, the debate of a topic such as Darwinian evolution. Likewise science should be used to foster creative writing skills and provide a context for technological problem solving. Such planning and design of provision, starting from a skills, competency and capability base, would do much to enhance science teaching, improve the relevance of scientific knowledge gained during courses of study and avoid a repetitious approach to skill development.

Given that course structures are likely to vary with local circumstances it will be essential to have a common framework for reporting achievement. The framework would need to include records of all three facets of provision discussed above, either in that form or perhaps in terms of the 'Common Learning Outcomes' favoured by the CBI. Either way we would wish to stress the importance of criterion-referenced assessment, formative as well as summative assessment, and a strong element of student self-assessment, which has been demonstrated to be a powerful motivating factor in educational and training programmes. A modular approach to the training facet would mean that a report of assessment in the form of a profile or record of achievement would have to specify the level of the module – NVQ level 2 or level 3 – and probably a descriptor of the content area. Universities or employers might then be able to specify their minimum requirements in terms of a certain number of modules at defined levels. They would also require some detail of achievement in the skills aspect of the preparation facet and the extent of the students' engagement in the developmental facet. If, however, the sort of pattern of post-16 work we have described became the norm, employers and others would know that all applicants would have automatically followed courses containing the broader elements of the curriculum we have outlined.

If the model of entitlement is accepted, and learning is seen to be a negotiated process between students and institutions, then flexibility may mean a large variety of methods of delivery with a common form of record of achievement providing appropriate continuity. It is, we feel, now widely acknowledged that records of achievement provide important feedback to students and empower them to take greater control over their learning. We believe this to be of particular importance, for under an entitlement curriculum students might be of any age and with varying aspirations and motivations. They may be in full- or part-time attendance at schools, colleges and centres, or be engaged in supported self-study on the Open College or Open University model. The system, to be effective, will need to foster and encourage mixed modes of attendance and allow study time extending over longer periods than our current system supports. In such a context individual 'learning access credits' that can be spent as, when and how individuals wish would be compatible with our proposals and might do much to increase the viability of schools with small sixth forms. In fact competition and cooperation between institutions, combined with flexibility by employers and higher education, might well result in the provision of an education service that builds on the National Curriculum by really catering for the complex needs of continuing education and training.

While appreciating the cost implications, we suggest that significant progress towards an entitlement curriculum for all 16–19-year-olds would be greatly facilitated by the increased flexibility that the introduction of a unified credit accumulation and transfer scheme, accrediting all vocational, academic and experiential learning, would bring. It would also be helpful if such a unified system of awards could be extended to cover the pre-16 curriculum. The Dorset/Oxfordshire Accreditation Project is making some progress towards this. This project was set up to investigate and develop a comprehensive system of certification from 14 to 19. To date the project has negotiated with partner examining and validation bodies a common format for submitting certification and accreditation proposals for approval. These systems, which incorporate academic/vocational linking, work-related education and cross-curricular programmes, are being tested through several pilot proposals. Perhaps our ultimate objective should be the development of a credit accumulation and transfer scheme that operates in a seamless way from 5 to 19. The NCC Core Skills document (NCC, 1990) really requires us to revisit our hastily prepared definition of pre-16 provision and provides the opportunity to be more radical. In this context the development of a full bottom-up 5–19 credit accumulation scheme with no artificial certification and access barriers at age 16 has much to offer and could create significant savings to offset some of the costs involved.

Important as it is to our vision of the future, we would not wish the issue of credit and credit accumulation to cloud, or inhibit, important developments that can and should take place within existing frameworks. A new structure for post-16 education, though vital, is not a ·prior condition for improving the *quality* of science teaching post-16. Much could be done, for example, by building into existing programmes the range of teaching and learning activities spelt out in *SATIS 16–19*:

> brainstorming; case studies; data analysis; designing; discussion; devising a poster; interpreting maps; listening to audio tapes; practical investigations; preparing and giving a talk; problem solving and decision making; reading; role play; surveys; watching and discussing videos; writing technical reports; writing for a non-specialist audience.
>
> (ASE, 1990)

To this impressive list we might add talking, listening, drama, dreaming, thought experiments and truly creative writing. We could also do much, as we have already suggested, through the introduction of alternative pedagogies linked to alternative patterns of attendance. Quality of provision could be further enhanced if we gave our 16–19-year-olds greater autonomy as students and enhanced their ability to negotiate their learning programmes. Finally, and by no means least, we must at all costs re-evaluate the relationship between knowledge, skills and work. In an important paper Spours and Young discuss the concept of a vocational model of general education. They describe five principles of Vocational Aspects of Academic Learning (the VAAL perspective):

(i)   Instead of starting with academic subjects and vocational programmes, it proposes a critical relationship between academic subjects and the changing nature of the world of work. This is in contrast to a vocationalised experientialism in which there is no concept of knowledge and to the academic subjects of the National Curriculum ossified by a renewed emphasis upon testing.

(ii) It recognises the central role of economic and technological understanding in the curriculum for all students from 14+.

(iii) It is a proposal for a general and vocational education for all pupils not just underachievers. It is therefore a new basis of a common secondary curriculum.

(iv) It is a perspective which encourages the development and renewal of existing academic subjects and their relationship to pupil experience as well as the development of new specialisations.

(v)   It is a perspective that incorporates a concept of future into its definitions of school knowledge, work and skill.

(Spours and Young, 1988)

In the search for greater relevance and linkage with the world of work we also need to ensure that education and training provide ample opportunities for people to meet the challenge of developing a sound knowledge and understanding of important intellectual, creative and aesthetic domains. We accept that it is only on this basis that we can seek to redefine existing subjects and specialisms with the degree of rigour we will need in the future. We regard as an exciting prospect the challenge to reshape, say, A-level courses to meet some or all of the criteria presented above, or better still, use these perspectives for the reconstruction of the educational system.

> Like Eastern semi-invalids in frontier days, Oppenheimer's encounter with wilderness, freeing him from overcivilized restraints, was decisive, a healing of faith. From an ill and perhaps hypochondriac boy he weathered across a vigorous summer to a physically confident young man. He arrived at Harvard tanned and fit, his body at least in shape. At Harvard he imagined himself a Goth coming into Rome. 'He intellectually looted the place,' a classmate says. He routinely took six courses for credit — the requirement was five — and audited four more. Nor were they easy courses. He was majoring in chemistry, but a typical year might include four semesters of chemistry, two of French literature, two of mathematics, one of philosophy and three of physics, these only the courses credited. He read on his own as well, studied languages, found occasional weekends for sailing the 27-foot sloop his father had given him or for all-night hikes with friends, wrote short stories and poetry when the spirit moved him but generally shied away from extracurricular activities and groups. Nor did he date; he was still unformed enough to brave no more than worshipping older women from afar. He judged later that 'although I liked to work, I spread myself very thin and got by with murder.' The murder he got by with resulted in a transcript solid with A's sprinkled with B's; he graduated *summa cum laude* in three years.
>
> (Rhodes, 1986)

REFERENCES

ASE (1989) *Post-16 Science Studies: The A and AS-Level Dimension.* Hatfield: Association for Science Education, for ASE/CNAA/SCUE.

ASE (1990) *SATIS 16–19 Project.* Hatfield: Association for Science Education.

Baker, Kenneth. Speech to the Association of Colleges of Further and Higher Education (ACFHE), February.

Bausor, J. and Zachary, D. (1990) A structure for post-16 education: some suggestions. Mimeo.

CBI (1989) *Towards a Skills Education*. London: Confederation of British Industry.

Education journal (1990) *Education*, **175**(16).

Engineering Council and Society of Education Officers (1988) *Advancing A-Levels*. London: Engineering Council and Society of Education Officers.

Foundation for Science and Technology (1987) *The Path to Higher Education: An Action Report*. London: Foundation for Science and Technology.

Higginson Report (1988) *Advancing A-Levels*. London: HMSO.

ILEA (1988) The way forward: an alternative route for post-16 science studies. London: ILEA/ASE/SSCR *ad hoc* group. Mimeo.

Institute of Physics (1990) *Report of the 16–19 Physics Course Working Party*. Bristol: Institute of Physics.

Policy Studies Institute (1990) *Britain's Real Skill Shortage*. London: Policy Studies Institute.

Rhodes, A. (1986) *The Making of the Atomic Bomb*. New York: Simon & Schuster.

Royal Society (1988) *The 16–19 Science Curriculum and Its Assessment: A Statement of Policy*. London: Royal Society.

Royal Society of Arts (1989) *Aim Higher: Widening Access to Higher Education*. London: Royal Society of Arts.

Royal Society of Arts (1990) *More Means Different: Widening Access to Higher Education*. London: Royal Society of Arts.

Secondary Heads Association (1989) *Planning 16–19 Education*. Leicester: Secondary Heads Association.

Smithers, A. and Robinson, P. (1989) *Increasing Participation in Higher Education*. London: British Petroleum, p. 3.

Spours, K. and Young, M. (1988) Beyond vocationalism: a new perspective on the relationship between work and education. Working Paper No. 4, Post-16 Education Centre, University of London Institute of Education.

West, R. W., Zachary, D. *et al.* (1989). A question of entitlement: a contribution to the post-16 debate. Mimeo.

Name Index

Armstrong, R. 10
Association for Science Education
(ASE) 106, 107, 112, 131, 150,
154, 169

Baker, Kenneth 155, 156
Bausor, J. 164
Baxter, J. 12
Beaver, S. H. 76
Bentley, D. 14, 116, 127
Bosch, Karl 98
Black, M. 73
Black, P. 8, 58, 59
Braham, M. 69, 83
Bruner, J. S. 72, 81

Carpenter, I. 77
Cassels, Sir John 154
Chadwick, James 152
Children's Learning in Science
Project (CLISP) 19
Confederation of British Industry
(CBI) 154, 166
Cornbleth, C. 69
Council for National Academic
Awards (CNAA) 154

d'Arcy, P. (Martin et al.) 50
Department of Education and
Science (DES) 1, 8, 11, 33, 35, 38,
62, 75, 76, 77, 78, 79–80, 103, 105,
126, 127, 128, 149
Dewey, J. 73

Ebbutt, D. 14
Eisner, E. 70, 73, 75, 80
Elliott, J. 72, 83
Engineering Council 154

Farmer, R. 9, 10
Foundation for Science and
Technology 154
Further Education Unit (FEU) 3

Galileo 92
Gardner, K. 47
Geographical Association 77
Gilbert, R. 76
Goodson, I. 73
Gordon, P. 80

Haber, Fritz 95-9
Harding, Sir Roy 154
Harrison, G. H. 8, 59
Her Majesty's Inspectorate (HMI)
89, 90, 91
Her Majesty's Stationery Office
(HMSO) 76, 84, 154
Hoborough, J. 10
Hoyle, P. 141
Hussey, M. 131

Inner London Education Authority
(ILEA) 139, 141, 154, 171
Institute of Physics (IOP) 154

Jarrett, J. R. 70, 83
Johnston, R. J. 73, 77

Subject Index